OTHER BOOKS BY GORDON DONALDSON

Scotland: Church and Nation through Sixteen Centuries

The Scottish Reformation

Shetland Life under Earl Patrick

The Making of the Scottish Prayer Book of 1637

Scotland: James V to James VII

The Scots Overseas

Mary, Queen of Scots

Scotland, The Shaping of a Nation

Scottish Historical Documents

A Source Book of Scottish History
(with W. Croft Dickinson)

A Short History of Scotland
(with R. L. Mackie)

Who's Who in Scottish History
(with R. S. Morpeth)

A Dictionary of Scottish History
(with R. S. Morpeth)

FORT BRAGG
9/29/88
MENDOCINO COUNTY LIBRARY
1000 09 176994 0 0
WITHDRA
D0709383
GENEALOGICAL COLLECTION
PROPERTY OF MENDOCINO COAST GENEALOGICAL SOCIETY

SCOTTISH KINGS

Gordon Donaldson

SCOTTISH KINGS

B. T. BATSFORD LTD
London

First published 1967

© Gordon Donaldson 1967

Second edition (revised) 1977

Made and printed in Great Britain by
J. W. Arrowsmith Ltd., Bristol
for the Publishers B. T. Batsford Ltd
4 Fitzhardinge Street, London W1H 0AH

ISBN 0 7134 1028 0

Contents

Acknowledgement

Figs 14, 15 and 26 are reproduced by gracious permission of Her Majesty The Queen. The author and publishers also wish to thank the following for the illustrations appearing in this book:

Aerofilms Limited for fig. 11; Trustees of The British Museum for figs 8 and 9; His Grace The Marquess of Bute for fig 18; The Master and Fellows of Corpus Christi College, Cambridge for fig 6; Edinburgh Central Public Library for fig. 34; Mansell Collection for fig 1; Ministry of Public Building and Works (Crown copyright reserved) for figs 10, 12, 20 and 25; National Gallery of Scotland for figs 14 and 15; National Library of Scotland for figs 7, 16 and 19; National Monuments Record of Scotland for fig. 24; *Radio Times* Hulton Picture Library for figs 2, 35 and 36; His Grace The Duke of Roxburghe for fig. 7; Scottish National Portrait Gallery for figs 17, 18, 22, 23, 27-30, 31 and 32; J. B. White, Ltd for fig. 21; Colonel William Stirling of Keir for fig. 17; Württembergische Landesbibliothek, Stuttgart for fig. 13.

Genealogical Tables

The Illustrations

1. Seal of King Edgar *From Anderson's 'Diplomata'*

1

The Early Scottish Monarchy

When the last of the male line of Scotland's native royal family was inaugurated as King Alexander III in 1249, all the actions in the ceremony revealed something of the meaning of Scottish kingship, and some of them amply illustrated its antiquity. The new King, we are told, was 'consecrated' by the Bishop of St Andrews. The association of the Church with the inauguration of a new king, and his hallowing in some way by the leading ecclesiastic of the kingdom, went back at least to the sixth century, when St Columba himself had laid his hand on Aidan and so 'ordained' him as King. But, apart from the 'consecration' by the Bishop the proceedings at the inauguration of Alexander III resembled primitive rites for the installation of a pagan tribal chief rather than the investiture of a Christian monarch of Western Europe in the high Middle Ages. The ceremony did not take place in a church, for Alexander was led into the open air, from the abbey church of Scone to the moot-hill nearby, and the central act was the setting of the King upon a stone which, though normally kept in the church, was taken out of doors for the occasion. It appears that by ancient tradition the privilege of setting the King on this stone belonged not to any prelate but to the Earl of Fife, who was recognised as the leading layman of the realm. Homage was rendered to the new monarch, and no doubt he took an oath, so that the reciprocal responsibilities of king and people were demonstrated. Then, when all else was over, a Highland bard bowed low before the new King and hailed him in Gaelic as 'Alexander, King of Alba, son of Alexander, son of William, son of Henry, son of David', and so recited his pedigree back to 'Fergus, the first King of the Scots in Scotland'.

The Scots could, in sober fact, trace their King's lineage with some authenticity back to a Fergus, the son of Erc, who had come from Ireland to settle with his people in Dalriada (Argyll) around the year 500. But a far greater antiquity than that was claimed for the royal line, and for the Scots themselves, in remarkable flights of fancy which suggest that Scotland's most gifted composer of fiction was a nameless propagandist who lived at some unknown date in the Middle Ages. It was related that the Scots derived their origin from Gaythelos (whence, allegedly, Gael), son of a King of Greece, who went to Egypt in the days of Moses. He married the eponymous Scota, daughter of Pharaoh, and led his family from Egypt to Spain. From that country several colonies of their descendants went to Ireland, the last of them under Simon Brek, and under Simon's grandson, so the story went on, the Scots passed over into northern Britain and gave the name of Scotia to that part of the island. In the year 330 BC the Scots who had thus settled in Scotland elected as their King Fergus, son of Ferehard, who was reckoned Fergus I and from whom the dynasty was dated. Under the rule of the line of Fergus the Scots remained in Scotland for seven centuries. In AD 360, however, after King Eugenius (Ewen) had been slain by the Picts and Britons, the Scots, under his brother Ethodius and his nephew Erc, were driven back to Ireland. Then in the fifth century they returned under Fergus, son of Erc, and reoccupied Argyll. From Fergus, son of Erc, the succession continued down to Kenneth, son of Alpin, who united the Picts with the Scots under his rule, in a kingdom called Alba (the territory north of the Forth and Clyde).

History knows nothing of any settlement of Scots in Scotland at any point earlier than about 500, but with Fergus, son of Erc, myth more or less connects with history, and Kenneth, son of Alpin, is authentic enough as the first King of the Picts and Scots.

The invention of the forty-five kings alleged to have ruled from Fergus, son of Ferehard, to Fergus, son of Erc, was designed to give the Scottish dynasty a startling lead in any contest based on claims to antiquity. It must be admitted that the Scots were outdone in imagination by the Irish, who were claiming in the fourteenth century to have had nearly 200 kings, but it is significant of much in the Scottish attitude to the monarchy that the Highland bard who recited Alexander III's pedigree in 1249 regarded him as the latest in a line of upwards of 100 kings.

Some versions of the legend related that the Scots had in all their wanderings taken with them a sacred stone, which, according to one account, had been the pillow on which the patriarch Jacob had slept when he had his miraculous dream at Bethel. On this stone, sometimes called a marble seat, the kings of the Scots had always been installed. It was said by some to have been for a time at Iona after it was brought from Ireland, and later legend placed it for a time also at Beregonium and Dunstaffnage, two fortresses on opposite sides of the mouth of Loch Etive in Argyll. After the union of the Picts and Scots it found its home at Scone.

At King Alexander III's inauguration, therefore, both the use of the stone and the recital of the pedigree placed him in continuity with a long past. But it is also necessary to note what was absent from the ceremonial. Only later accounts (coloured by later practice) say that he was crowned, and, although the Scottish kings are depicted as wearing a crown at least from the time of Edgar (1097–1107), there is no contemporary evidence that the placing of a crown on the king's head had yet, in Alexander III's time, become part of the rite of inauguration. The stone of Scone was not yet a 'coronation stone'. If there was no crowning, it was even more significant that there was no anointing. This sacramental action, the most sacred and most Christian part of a coronation ceremony, had not yet been introduced to Scotland. The fact was that unction was the mark of full and independent sovereignty, and the persistent English claims to superiority over the Scottish kings had made the status of the latter somewhat ambiguous. Therefore, when the Scots craved from the pope recognition of their right to anoint (as well as crown) their kings, they met with refusal. The pope, although he did not yield to the English demand that he should explicitly forbid the anointing or crowning of Scottish kings, had given way to English pressure to the extent of declining to concede the right to be crowned and anointed.

King Alexander III, like his predecessors for perhaps three and a half centuries, was inaugurated at Scone, which had become something of a centre of the Scottish monarchy not long after Kenneth, son of Alpin, united the Picts and Scots. But he was not buried in Iona, the ancient burial place of Scottish—and other—kings; the abandonment of Iona as a burial place reflected the profound changes which had begun to come over the Scottish monarchy and the life of the Scottish people since the eleventh century. King Malcolm II (1005–34) had been the first king to rule over a kingdom which reached beyond the old bounds of Alba and extended to the Tweed and the Solway. It therefore included the English-speaking peoples of south-eastern Scotland and the Welsh-speaking Britons of the south-west, both of them elements alien to the old Scoto-Pictish realm north of the Forth and Clyde. Tension arose between native influence on one hand and external, southern influence on the other, and is illustrated in the history of the succession to the throne.

In so far as there can be said to have been a rule of succession in Alba, it was that the eldest, or ablest, male of the royal house, and not the heir of line, should inherit the throne, but this meant that any energetic male could assert his claim, which he often did by encompassing the death of the reigning sovereign. It was later believed that Malcolm II's father, Kenneth II, had tried to ensure his son's succession by altering the old system, but if he made such an attempt it met with opposition, for on Kenneth's death two kinsmen excluded Malcolm from the throne for a time. Malcolm, however, succeeded in bringing about the installation after him of his grandson Duncan—Shakespeare's Duncan—contrary to the old rules, but Duncan's position was challenged by Macbeth, who, by the native principles, had a dual claim to the throne, both in his own right and in that of his wife. Macbeth's success against Duncan, whom he defeated and killed in battle, thus represented a native, or Celtic, reaction against the new southern ways, and it is significant of the prevailing distrust of those ways that he was able to rule with evident acceptance for seventeen years. He was finally ousted not because of a rising among his own people but because Malcolm Canmore, son of Duncan, had taken refuge in England and found an English, or at least Northumbrian, army to support his claims. Macbeth was defeated and killed, and Duncan's son became King Malcolm III. Macbeth, who had represented the old ways, was buried in Iona like his predecessors, but Malcolm III and his English wife, Margaret, when they died in 1093, were buried at Dunfermline. Malcolm had made that place his headquarters in preference to the earlier seats of Scottish and Pictish royalty at Dunkeld, Scone and Abernethy, and Margaret had introduced Benedictine monks to the church there, under the influence of Lanfranc, Archbishop of Canterbury.

The native cause was not yet lost, for on the death of Malcolm and Margaret a Celtic reaction was again effective enough to put Donald Bane, Malcolm's brother, on the throne for a brief space. Donald had spent his boyhood not in England, like Malcolm, but in the Western Isles, and he has been characterised as an 'incorrigible old Celt'.* Once again, however, southern armed force was called in, to put the sons of Malcolm on the throne, and the aged Donald, taken prisoner and blinded, was set to work in the laundry. 'But Celtic royalty was indefeasible. Donald Bane might be old, and blind, and take in washing, but when he died he was buried in the sacred island where Kenneth mac Alpin lay, with all the Scottish kings around him.'† But Donald was the last king to be buried in Iona. The sons of Malcolm and Margaret and their descendants pursued an Anglicising and Normanising policy and Dunfermline became the usual royal burying-place. A great

*R. L. Graeme Ritchie, *The Normans in Scotland* (Edinburgh University Press, 1954), 64

†*Ibid.*, 87

abbey was erected there in the twelfth century and the sanctity of the place was exalted when Queen Margaret, whose shrine was there, was canonised in 1250.

The dynasty to which Margaret's descendants, down to Alexander III, belonged is often called the House of Canmore, almost as if Canmore had been the surname of Malcolm III and not merely a personal epithet meaning 'big-head'. But a royal house is usually named after its male progenitor, and according to that practice a more suitable name would be the House of Dunkeld, because the family sprang from Malcolm Canmore's grandfather, Crinan, Abbot of Dunkeld, who had married a daughter of Malcolm II. That term would emphasise its native roots. The term 'House of Canmore' does emphasise, properly enough, that new elements entered into Scottish government and society with Canmore and his descendants, but such an emphasis could be even more appropriately given if, departing from the usual practice, we spoke of those kings as 'the Margaretsons', for it was the English Margaret who impressed so many of her views and aims on her sons and descendants. None of her six sons was given a Scottish Christian name, and among the kings of the house only one—Malcolm IV—had a Scottish Christian name. They had, of course, no surname, but it was characteristic of their whole position and outlook that one of them, known to Scottish historians as William the Lion, was most readily identified among his contemporaries as Guillaume de Varenne, from his mother's territorial designation. It was remarked in 1212 that 'the more recent kings of Scots profess themselves to be rather Frenchmen [*i.e.*, Normans], both in race and in manners, language and culture, and . . . they admit only Frenchmen to their friendship and service'.

The royal house, however named, sprang on its native side from the kings of the Scots, who had been only one of the four or five peoples inhabiting the bounds of modern Scotland, and possibly the least numerous of them. Yet, first of all when Kenneth, son of Alpin, united the Picts and the Scots, and later when the Anglian south-east and the British south-west were incorporated into the kingdom, the royal line of the Scots seems to have been accepted without difficulty by the other peoples. The pretenders who from time to time contested the claims of the Margaretsons were themselves members of the Scottish royal family. The remarkable fact is that not only the royal line, but the whole history—and mythology—of the Scots was accepted as the heritage of all the people from the Tweed to the Pentland Firth. By the reign of Alexander III, it is clear, Picts and Britons, Scandinavians, Angles and Normans had all alike laid aside their own particular memories of the past and had come to regard the past of the Scots as their heritage. As the kingship symbolised this acceptance of a common past, it was an important unifying factor in Scottish life. It was, indeed, one of the few things contributed by West Highland Scotland to the Scottish state, and one of the few things which linked the Highlanders with the Lowlanders. It must have astonished some contemporaries when the Highland bard, at the inauguration of Alexander III, hailed this Anglicised, French-speaking king as the descendant of Fergus I.

The descent of the Margaretsons was not in dispute; but if they owed their throne to their descent, it was not so clear that they owed it to the strict observance of the rule of primogeniture. Malcolm Canmore's own success against Macbeth had been an assertion of that rule, in distinction from the older principles of succession, but the rule of primogeniture did not justify the succession of Malcolm's sons by Margaret. Malcolm had children by an earlier marriage; the eldest of them had actually reigned as Duncan II for a few months in 1094, and for generations his descendants contested the claims of the descendants of Margaret. The latter could appeal to the principle of primogeniture against the line of Duncan II only by alleging—without real foundation—that Duncan had been illegitimate. Edgar, the first of the sons of Malcolm and Margaret to reign as king of Scots, was placed on the throne by an English army sent by the English King, and his accession was simply a case of conquest with foreign assistance. From Edgar onwards, primogeniture was followed within the Margaretson line. The unmarried Edgar was followed by his brother Alexander I, who had no legitimate issue, and Alexander in turn by the youngest brother, David. David's son predeceased him, and the next King was David's grandson, Malcolm IV, a boy of twelve, whose accession marked a clear success for primogeniture. Malcolm, who died unmarried, was followed by his brother William, and thereafter Alexander II and Alexander III each succeeded his father. Alexander III was predeceased by his sons and his daughter, leaving as his heir of line his granddaughter Margaret, 'the Maid of Norway', daughter of a marriage between Alexander's daughter and the King of Norway. It is significant of the triumph of primogeniture that in 1286 this girl, at the age of less than four, was accepted as heiress to the Scottish throne, though the step was logical enough in view of the undeviating practice ever since the Margaretsons had come to the throne.

Throughout the twelfth and thirteenth centuries, therefore, from the accession of Edgar in 1097, the Scottish succession had been conspicuously regular. In England, in the same period, the rule of primogeniture had frequently been violated. William II and Henry I had both become Kings to the exclusion of their elder brother, Robert; Stephen, a nephew of Henry I, succeeded in place of Henry's daughter Matilda; and John succeeded Richard I although Prince Arthur was the son of an elder brother. The first clear triumph for primogeniture in England was the acceptance of Henry III, a minor, as successor to his father John.

English example, very familiar to the Scots, showed that primogeniture would not necessarily prevail, and the Scottish succession itself, although it had shown a strictly hereditary character in practice, also retained an element which, if not actually elective, certainly recalled the usages of the earlier days before primogeniture was established. David I, not confident that his son Henry would succeed him without challenge, caused him to be styled *rex designatus* or King-designate; and when Henry after all predeceased his father, his son Malcolm was then formally proclaimed heir to his grandfather. William the Lion was long without a son, and it was later said that when, in 1195, he proposed to designate his daughter as his heir, he was opposed by the Scottish magnates, who thought that a nephew should be preferred to a daughter. Again, in 1238, so it was alleged, when Alexander II was still without a son, a 'parliament' declared Robert Bruce, Lord of Annandale, who was the nearest male in the royal line, to be heir, to the exclusion of females. If those transactions took place in 1195 and 1238, it is easy to understand why in 1284 Alexander III wished to obtain from the magnates of his realm a formal undertaking to accept as his successor his granddaughter, the Maid of Norway. What it all suggests is a concept, if not of election, at least of something like what we should now call a statutory succession.

More generally, the Scottish kingship was not solely a personal or dynastic kingship. Far more important than the rights of a single individual or a single family was the concept of the inviolable integrity of the nation, of which the kingship was the symbol. Soon after the death of Alexander III events showed how clearly and tenaciously the idea was held that the nation and the state had an existence apart from any personal monarch. When Alexander died in 1286, his grandaughter was entitled to succeed by the declaration of 1284. In order to maintain the cohesion of the country and carry on the administration, six 'Guardians'—two earls, two bishops and two barons—were 'appointed by common counsel' or 'chosen by the community of the realm'. By this time men had long been accustomed to see as the symbol and instrument of administration a King's seal, depicting the sovereign enthroned on one side and the sovereign on horseback on the other. For the use of the Guardians there was now produced an impersonal great seal, depicting the lion rampant, the armorial bearings of the King of Scots, on one side, and St Andrew, the patron saint of Scotland, on the other. Here, plain to see, was an expression of belief in the nation and state of Scotland, even when the sovereign was a little girl across the sea in Norway.

The concept was to be severely tried in the next two decades. The Maid of Norway died on her way to Scotland in 1290, leaving

THE HOUSE OF DUNKELD

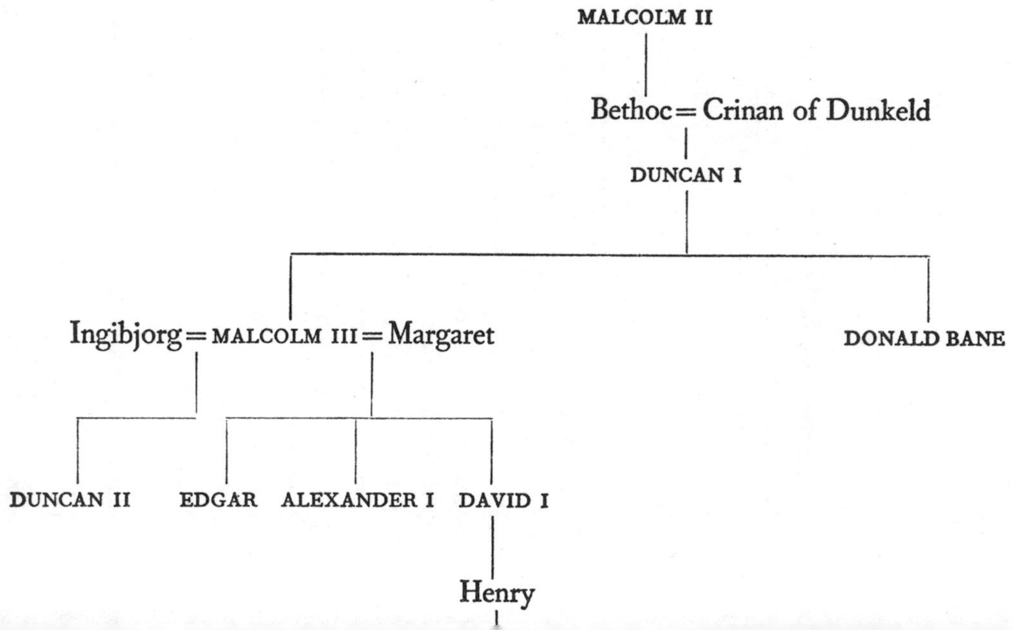

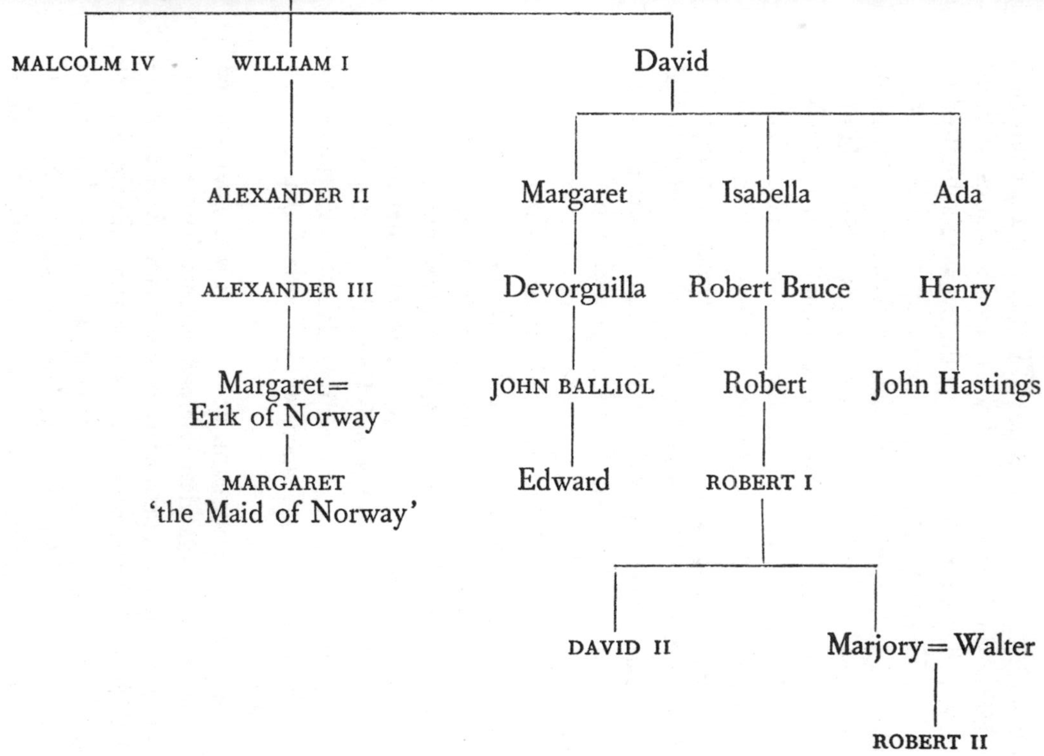
MALCOLM IV
WILLIAM I
David
ALEXANDER II
ALEXANDER III
Margaret=
Erik of Norway
MARGARET
'the Maid of Norway'
Margaret
Devorguilla
JOHN BALLIOL
Edward
Isabella
Robert Bruce
Robert
ROBERT I
DAVID II
Marjory=Walter
ROBERT II
Ada
Henry
John Hastings

the realm without even a titular head. The Guardians continued to rule during the interregnum. The competing claims of those who thought they were entitled to the throne were submitted to Edward I of England, whose insistence that he should first be acknowledged as overlord of Scotland met with protests not from the competitors or from individual magnates but from those who spoke for what they called 'the community of the realm'. Edward's adjudication was in favour of John Balliol. Balliol's ancestor, Guy de Bailleul, a Picard, had been a landowner in England under William Rufus; Guy's son, Bernard, had appeared in Scotland under David I; and John Balliol's grandfather had married the eldest niece of William the Lion. On the principles of primogeniture, which the Scottish succession had so long followed and on which Edward's own tenure of the English throne was based, John Balliol had the best right. Balliol, like his predecessors, was inaugurated by being set upon the stone at Scone—the last king to be so installed in Scotland; the Earl of Fife was a minor at the time, and King Edward nominated one John of Perth to take his place at the ceremony. After four years, Balliol, or Balliol's people, found Edward's overlordship intolerable, but the consequence was that Balliol was deposed by Edward and dismissed to France, while Scotland was overrun by the English.

During this new interregnum, government was again carried on and resistance to England maintained by Guardians and others on behalf of 'the whole community of the realm'. Andrew Murray and William Wallace, when they temporarily liberated most of Scotland from English occupation in 1297, described themselves as leaders of 'the army of the kingdom of Scotland' and also professed to act in name of the community of the realm. They did not repudiate the title of Balliol and acknowledge that his forced abdication had been binding, but the concept of a *de jure* 'King over the water' does not seem at this stage to have been strong enough for them to feel that it was sufficient to use the name of the absent King John. After the defeat of Wallace at Falkirk (1298), there were once more Guardians, described as 'appointed by the community of the realm' and as acting 'with the whole community of the realm', and they maintained resistance to the English until 1305. It was characteristic of the current concept that when Edward demanded that the Earl of Angus should give up the castles of Forfar and Dundee, Angus refused, on the ground that they had been entrusted to him by 'the community of the realm of Scotland'.

The 'community' was not, of course, the 'commonalty' or 'the commons' in the modern sense of that term; nor was it the entire nation. But it is harder to define it positively. It is sometimes equated with the *bon gens* or *probi homines*, which might mean men of substance, or might mean men who were neither of servile status nor of criminal character. At any rate, we should not be far wrong if we identify the 'community' with what we should now call the responsible men of the land, the politically active, or politically conscious, citizens. There is no particular mystique about the term, nor was its use peculiar to the realm of Scotland or restricted to realms in general. One hears, for example, of 'the community of the Isle of Man' in the late thirteenth century, of 'the community of the county of Lothian' in 1335, and of 'the communities' of the English shires of Cumberland, Northumberland and Durham. The last three are so styled when they paid a kind of blackmail to the Scottish King to relieve them from his marauding raids, and in that context 'the community' might almost mean the taxpayers or ratepayers.

If the constant references to 'the community of the realm of Scotland' do mean that the politically conscious classes in the kingdom felt aware of their cohesion, as subjects of a state, even when the realm was without a king, there are traces also of a continuing belief in a kind of impersonal crown, distinct from the person of the monarch. This had been illustrated by the appearance of the lion rampant on the seal of the Guardians in 1286, and in 1304, when the realm was again without a king, the defenders of Stirling Castle against the English declared that their allegiance was to 'the Lion'.

2

The House of Bruce and the Accession of the Stewarts

The family of Bruce, initially de Brus, took its name from Brix in the Cotentin, near the western extremity of Normandy. From there, Robert de Brus accompanied his Duke, William the Conqueror, on his expedition to England in 1066. It was another Robert, grandson of this Bruce of the Conquest, who founded the family's fortunes in Scotland. He was in high favour with Henry I of England, from whom he held wide estates in Yorkshire, and at Henry's court he became known to the Scottish Prince David, youngest son of Malcolm and Margaret and brother-in-law of the English King. David evidently decided that Bruce would be a reliable agent in Scotland, and shortly after his accession to the Scottish throne in 1124 he granted to Bruce the lands of Annandale, extending to some 200,000 acres. Bruce, like many another, was thus a feudal vassal of the Scottish crown as well as the English, and the potential difficulties inherent in such a position became manifest in 1138, when David went to war with King Stephen and invaded England. The Lord of Annandale formally renounced his allegiance to David before the Scottish and English armies met at the battle of the Standard, but his son remained in the Scottish army—and was taken prisoner by his father. There may well have been collusion to produce such a satisfactory outcome. At any rate, the son who had remained on the Scottish side succeeded to the English as well as the Scottish estates of the family, and lived until 1194. His grandson married Isabella, second daughter of David, Earl of Huntingdon, the younger brother of Malcolm IV and William the Lion.

It was this marriage which brought the Bruce family into the royal succession and gave them prospects of the crown, at a time when the direct male descent was extremely tenuous. Malcolm IV was unmarried, William the Lion was survived by only one son, Alexander II, who had no issue when his first wife died early in 1238. Alexander's cousin, John, the only surviving son of David, Earl of Huntingdon, had died in 1237 without issue. A need to settle the succession was urgent, and in 1238, so at least the Bruces later claimed, it was agreed that Robert Bruce, son of the Princess Isabella, second daughter of Earl David, should succeed in preference to the daughter of Isabella's elder sister. Before Alexander II died in 1249, he had a son, who succeeded as Alexander III, and it seemed that nothing more might be heard of the Bruce claim. In 1284 Bruce acknowledged the Maid of Norway as heir to the throne, and in 1289 he was one of the Scottish plenipotentiaries for the Treaty of Salisbury, in which Margaret was styled 'true lady, queen and heir' of Scotland. When, however, the succession to the throne became an open question after the death of the Maid in 1290, Robert Bruce claimed to be the rightful heir, although there was now a male representative of the line of his mother's elder sister, in the person of John Balliol. It was the latter who became King, by Edward I's decision, but when old Bruce, 'the Competitor', died in 1294 his claims were inherited by his son and then by his grandson. The son, who had become Earl of Carrick by marrying Marjory, daughter and heir of the last Celtic Earl of Carrick, lived until 1304, but he had resigned the earldom to his son some years before. Carrick, elder, and Carrick, younger, as they may be called—they were the seventh and eighth members of the family to have the Christian name Robert—played a tortuous part in Anglo-Scottish relations for several years. They could hardly have been expected to commit themselves to the cause of Scottish independence as long as it was also the cause of their rival John Balliol, and they vacillated between collaboration with Edward I and support of the Guardians who acted on behalf of 'the community of the realm of Scotland'. There are even indications that the father and son repeated the collusion which their ancestors had practised at the time of the battle of the Standard and deliberately took opposite sides for a time so that the family interest should be secure whether the native cause or the English cause prevailed. It seems that they were quite willing to hold the Scottish kingship as vassals of Edward should he agree to confer it upon them, and it was noticeable that whenever the return of Balliol seemed a possibility the Bruces were more disposed to come to terms with Edward.

In 1305 King Edward, after completing the conquest of Scotland, prepared an Ordinance for the government of the 'land' (not 'kingdom') of Scotland. This seemed to extinguish the Bruce prospect of achieving kingship through Edward, but even so it has never been determined why, at a time when Scottish resistance had to all appearances been finally crushed, the younger Carrick should suddenly choose what seems a singularly inopportune moment to launch a new rising against the English and pronounce himself King Robert I. The sacred stone had been removed from Scone to Westminster by Edward I after he deposed Balliol, but Bruce's followers gathered at the traditional scene of royal inaugurations at Scone. The blessing of the church was not wanting, for there were Scottish churchmen patriotic enough to defy not only Edward of England but also the pope, who at this time was supporting the English claims. The robes for the occasion were made in the sacristy of Glasgow Cathedral, and the Bishop of Glasgow brought to Scone 'the banner of Scotland' which he had hidden carefully away to save it from the English. No doubt the new King took an oath, and no doubt he received the homage of his supporters. But the only recorded rite was the placing on his head of a circlet of gold—a *coronella* or *coronetta*—by Isabella, Countess of Buchan, sister of the Earl of Fife (who was himself in English custody at the time). The whole ceremonial was maimed, but it represented an attempt to combine ancient tradition—the choice of Scone and the presence of a member of the noble family of Fife—with the newer feature of coronation, which was a substitute for enthronement on the Stone but was also expressive of a claim to independent sovereignty.

To some, however, Bruce looked like a usurper. John Balliol lived until 1313 and, even admitting that his extorted abdication was valid, he had a son, Edward, who had the best claim by primogeniture. It is a fact worth remembering that by what later become Jacobite principles the Bruce family, from whom the Stewarts derived their right to be Kings, would never have been on the throne at all, and that they had a competitor in a 'king over the water'. Bruce's claim to be king could be justified in fact—and was magnificently justified in fact—by his success in recovering the country from the English and inflicting on them the resounding defeat of Bannockburn. But a justification in law could come only by a kind of retrospective legalisation of his action in dispossessing the senior line. Such legalisation was furnished by a remarkable series of documents which implied or asserted the right of the community of the realm of Scotland to choose a king. At a parliament which Bruce held at St Andrews in March 1309, solemn declarations in his favour were approved by the prelates and the barons. The story they told was that Balliol had been forced on the Scots by Edward I against a general preference for the claims of the Bruces and that the people of the land, in revulsion against the miseries brought on them in consequence of Balliol's reign, had taken Robert Bruce for their King and had raised him to the throne. Any contrary claims, based on documents 'sealed in the past and containing the consent of the people', were dismissed on the ground that such documents had been obtained by force and fear. Not only was Balliol disregarded, but Bruce was declared the heir of Alexander III, to the exclusion of the Maid of Norway, apparently on the ground of the alleged declaration in favour of the Bruces in 1238 but in defiance of the fact that Bruce 'the Competitor' had acknowledged Margaret's claim in 1284 and 1289.

The clerical declaration in favour of King Robert seems to have been twice reissued later, and the adherence to him of the magnates was reaffirmed and elaborated in the 'Declaration of Arbroath', a letter sent to the pope in 1320 by a large number of nobles and barons and 'the whole community of the realm'. This declaration recited the mythical origins of the Scots, though it made no specific reference to Egypt and Greece and said only that the Scots had come from the parts of Scythia through the Mediterranean to Ireland and then to Scotland, where they had repulsed Angles, Britons and Picts and had maintained their independence under 113 native kings. From the violence of the English they had been rescued by King Robert, who was their chosen captain and led them like a Joshua or a Maccabeus. But the emphasis was on choice rather than on any right of blood, for they asserted that should Bruce give up the struggle they would set him aside and make another King, 'because so long as a hundred of us remain alive we will never be subject to the English'.

Possibly the reader of those declarations in favour of King Robert may sense that those who wrote them protested too much, and it would be easy to exaggerate the unanimity which there really was behind Bruce. It is a startling fact that five of the barons who set their seals to the Declaration of Arbroath's emphatic assertion of Bruce's leadership of the nation were, within a few months, on trial for treason. Possibly the initiative in the Declaration was taken not, as it bears to be, by the barons, but by a King seeking to create patriotic unity. If so, his politic effort achieved all too little, and his apprehensions were justified soon after his own death in 1329, for when Edward Balliol claimed the throne—and was actually crowned at Scone—he enjoyed for a brief space a remarkable amount of support.

The element of choice, the concept of something like a statutory title to the throne, emerges not only in the declarations in favour of Robert I, but also in the arrangements made for the succession after him. Until late in his life, Bruce had no lawful child save a daughter, Marjory, and in April 1315 it was declared in a parliament at Ayr that should the King die without a son the throne was to go, with Marjory's consent, to Edward Bruce, the King's brother, on the ground that he was 'a man of vigour and great skill in war for the defence of the rights and liberties of the Scottish realm'. After Edward were to come his male heirs, and Marjory was to succeed only should Edward, also, die without male heirs. It was further provided that, should Robert, Edward and Marjory all die without heirs, the leaders of the community were to take counsel for the choice of another king. Little more than three years later, Edward Bruce was dead, and Marjory also was dead, but she had married Walter, the Steward of Scotland, and in 1316 had given birth to a son, Robert. A parliament at Scone in 1318 therefore declared that, should King Robert die without male heirs, Robert, son of the Steward, was to succeed.

The family to which the throne was thus destined in the event of the failure of the male line of the house of Bruce traced their ancestry to a Breton family who had held the office of *dapifer*, or steward, to the archbishops of Dol, a place near Mont-St-Michel and only some seventy miles from Brix, where the Bruces originated. The first of the family to appear in Britain was Flaald, a son of one of those Breton stewards, who was presumably brought across the Channel by King Henry I and who held lands in Norfolk and Shropshire early in the twelfth century. Later Stewart genealogists, not content with the family's authentic antiquity and desirous of giving the royal house a native origin, looked back to the dim and misty eleventh century, when, so it was related, Macbeth had a companion, Banquo, to whom the witches on the heath had prophesied that 'you sall never be king, bot of ye sall cum mony kingis quhilkis be lang progressioun sall rejose the croun of Scotland'.* Banquo, it was recalled, had had a son, Fleance, who had escaped when Macbeth murdered his father, and the genealogists identified the historical

*This is the version in Bellenden's translation of the *History of Scotland* by Hector Boece

Flaald with the mythical Fleance. Flaald was succeeded in his estates by Alain, or Alan, and this Alan's second son, Walter FitzAlan, became David I's *dapifer* or steward in Scotland. He was endowed with lands in Renfrewshire, he founded Paisley Abbey, and in 1158 the office of Steward of Scotland was made hereditary in his family. His descendants played their parts in Scottish affairs throughout the thirteenth century: Walter, the third High Steward, was a justiciar of Scotland in 1230; Alexander, the fourth, was a regent in the minority of Alexander III and commanded the right wing of the Scottish army which drove the Norwegians back at the battle of Largs in 1263; and James, the fifth, was closely associated with Wallace and Bruce in the cause of Scottish independence. Walter, the sixth High Steward, who was born in 1292, succeeded his father, James, in 1309 and was one of the commanders of the Scottish army at Bannockburn. It was he who married Marjory Bruce in 1315. He died in 1326.

However, although Robert Stewart, the son of Walter and Marjory, had been declared heir presumptive in 1318, the accession of the house of Stewart was long deferred. King Robert I did not, after all, die without male heirs, for his son, David, was born in 1324 and succeeded in 1329. David came to a kingdom whose full independence had been acknowledged by England in the Treaty of Edinburgh-Northampton in 1328. The Scottish request for the return of the stone of Scone from Westminster had not, indeed, been successful, but King Robert had taken steps to secure for the monarchy something better than that hoary relic. He had sent ambassadors to the pope with a request that the Scottish Kings might be anointed and crowned. The papal bull granting this privilege reached Scotland only after the liberator King was dead, but it was in time for the inauguration of David II, who was thus the first Scottish King to be solemnly crowned and anointed. Bruce's *coronella* of 1306 had fallen into English hands and had gone the way of the earlier insignia of Scottish royalty, but no doubt King Robert had commissioned the making of a more splendid crown—which, enriched by the spoils of Bannockburn, he could well afford. A small sceptre was specially made for the hands of the seven-year-old David when he was anointed and crowned at Scone in 1331.

The pope, in his bull acceding to King Robert's request, had emphasised that unction conferred a special grace, just as the Holy Spirit had descended on Saul and David when they were anointed as Kings of Israel, but the interest of the Scots may have been less theological than practical: they wanted it to be demonstrated beyond any doubt that their Kings were now fully sovereign. They had sought unction in vain before the War of Independence, and when, in 1291, one of the claimants to the throne after the death of the Maid of Norway had argued that Scotland was not a sovereign kingdom, but an ordinary feudal fief divisible among heiresses, his lawyers had made much of the fact that Scottish Kings were not crowned or anointed like independent sovereigns. The value which King Robert put on unction is amply shown by the fact that in 1329 he was prepared to pay to the pope the very considerable sum of £2,000 for the privilege which he craved. That the Scots appreciated the value and significance of the anointing became evident again later in David II's reign. Among various proposals which were made to settle Anglo-Scottish relations on a permanent and peaceful footing there was one that after the death of David, who was childless, one king should rule both England and Scotland, with separate coronations in each country, but the critics of this plan pointed out that the King could be anointed only once and that the Scottish ceremony of inauguration would thus be defective or at any rate inferior to the English. The anointing of the King, like the ordination of a priest, could not be repeated.

Although David II was only five at his accession, his reign started with apparently favourable prospects. The full sovereignty of his kingdom had been recognised by both the King of England and the pope, peace existed between Scotland and England, and David himself was married to Joanna, sister of the English King. Disasters, however, soon crowded on the Scottish realm. King Robert's most trusted lieutenants did not long survive their master, and a country with a boy-King and an untried governor had to face a challenge from Edward Balliol, the son of the late King John. Balliol was supported initially by 'the Disinherited', those Anglo-Scottish landowners who had taken the English side against Bruce and had lost their Scottish lands in consequence, and at a later stage he was assisted by Edward III and English armies. The conduct of Scottish affairs in the crisis was inept, perhaps partly because King Robert's success had spread among his people a disregard of caution and even a kind of recklessness, but it was also true that the nation was divided and that the hereditary and statutory rights of David II commanded only limited support. For a time the English conquest of Scotland was once more almost complete, Edward Balliol was crowned at Scone in 1332, and in 1334 King David was sent to France for safety. In a desperate situation, with an absent boy-King, the Scots who adhered to the national cause again drew inspiration from their belief in an impersonal kingship, and in 1336 Edward III was complaining of Scots who 'asserted that they held of the Lion and of none other'. A second war of independence had to be waged to free the land again from English occupation.

By 1341 it was safe for King David to return, but in 1346, on an invasion of England, he was captured at the battle of Neville's Cross. The English remembered it as one of their country's achievements that

> *When all her chivalry hath been in France*
> *And she a mourning widow of her nobles,*
> *She hath herself not only well defended,*
> *But taken, and impounded as a stray,*
> *The King of Scots.**

David remained a prisoner in England for eleven years, and was liberated only on an undertaking by the Scots to pay a ransom of 100,000 merks.† David was childless, and on more than one occasion he was a party to negotiations whereby the Scottish crown was to pass on his death to the English King or an English prince, but the Scottish parliament rejected such proposals.

**Henry V*, Act I, scene ii

†Merk or Mark = 13*s.* 4*d.*

David, it would now appear, has been too severely censured for his part in the troubles of his reign. He was bound to be compared, to his disadvantage, with his father. But it is less than equitable to applaud King Robert's invasions of the north of England, which happened to be successful, and at the same time to regard David's expedition in 1346, which happened to be unsuccessful, as an unwarranted act of folly. Likewise, David's attempts to secure a negotiated settlement with England which, at the cost of sharing the English royal line, would have freed Scotland from the burden of the ransom and would have brought her many other advantages (including the return of the stone of Scone), were not indefensible, and the statesmanship of some of the terms proposed compares not unfavourably with those ultimately arrived at when Scotland and England entered into union in 1707. Besides, King Robert had himself been a party to the marriage of David to the sister of Edward III, and this had carried with it the possibility that one prince would succeed peacefully to both realms. It was further to David's disadvantage in the eyes of posterity that chroniclers who wrote during the reigns of the Stewart Kings who succeeded him were not disposed to enlarge on the failings of Robert the Steward, the first of that dynasty, although he had in truth played a shabby enough part in David's reign, and successive writers preferred instead to enlarge on the faults of David. Even recent historians have been afflicted with the same bias: one of them has remarked of David that 'It would have been better for Scotland if David Bruce, who was born too late, had never been born at all'*—so that Scotland might have had the blessings of Stewart rule from 1329 instead of only from 1371. Apart from the question—admittedly a complex one—whether David II or Robert the Steward showed more statesmanship and patriotism, the partiality of historians emerges in the accounts given of their private lives: David is reproached for his amorous adventures; but the dozen or more bastards of Robert the Steward, if they are mentioned at all, are described as stalwarts who were an asset to their father in his old age.

*G. W. S. Barrow, *Robert Bruce*, 413

David II died in 1371, and his nephew, the Steward, succeeded him with a statutory title under the Act of Succession of 1318. But there was nothing sacrosanct about a statute, and a parliament could conceivably have overturned the act of 1318 and declared in favour of another claimant. It is related that Robert II's right was contested by the Earl of Douglas, and in this there is no improbability; but the suggestion that Douglas regarded the marriage of his son and heir to one of the King's daughters as a suitable consolation prize is less convincing, for Douglas may well have regarded the Steward as his inferior rather than even his equal. If Robert's accession did not go wholly unchallenged it would indicate that his elevation to the throne was not unanimously admitted by families which rivalled the Stewarts in wealth and power.

It was, at any rate, necessary to define the succession after Robert II (who was already a man of fifty-five when he became King), and no time was lost in taking the first step in this direction. On 27 March 1371, the day after he had been crowned and anointed at Scone, the King, with the consent of the prelates, earls, nobles and great men of his kingdom, declared that on his death his eldest son, John, Earl of Carrick and Steward of Scotland, should succeed him on the throne. Almost exactly two years later, in a parliament held at Scone on 4 April 1373, a much more elaborate act of succession, amounting to an entail of the crown, was passed with the consent of 'the prelates, earls, barons and the rest of the chief men and nobles and of all others of the three estates or communities of the whole realm there assembled'. The crown was now destined to pass successively to John, Earl of Carrick, and his heirs male, whom failing to the King's second son, Robert, Earl of Fife and Menteith, and his heirs male, whom failing to Alexander, Lord of Badenoch, the King's third son, and his heirs male, whom failing to David, Earl of Strathearn, the King's fourth son, and his heirs male, whom failing to Walter, youngest son of the King, and his heirs male; 'and the foresaid five brothers and their heirs male descending from them happening finally and wholly to fail (which God forbid), the true and lawful heirs of the royal blood and kin shall thenceforward succeed to the kingdom and the right of reigning'. It is curious, and significant of the force attached to statute rather than blood, that, although the crown had come to the Stewarts through a female, it was now laid down that it was not to be transmitted through a female, except possibly on the extinction of all the male lines descended from Robert II. In fact, as will appear, the male line of the first of the five sons continued in unbroken, though tenuous, succession until the death of James V in 1542. But at that point (when, as it happened, the male lines of all the other sons of Robert II had long died out), the crown went not to any male but to the late King's infant daughter, Mary, Queen of Scots.

The necessity for the statute of 1373 had, however, been urgent at the time, for there was some doubt about the legitimacy of Robert II's children by his first wife, Elizabeth Mure, to whom he was related within the degrees forbidden by canon law. In 1347 they received a papal dispensation for their marriage, but their eldest son had been born before the dispensation was obtained, and their other two sons who were later to be mentioned in the entail of the crown had also been born before their parents were lawfully married. The dispensation expressly legitimated issue already born as well as those to be born, and by canon law children born before their parents' marriage were normally legitimated by subsequent wedlock. But this was only one of many instances when no dispensation could succeed in removing all doubts about the legitimacy of children who, according to canon law, had been born in incest. Despite the declarations of 1371 and 1373 sufficient uncertainty remained to give colour to the view that the descendants of Robert II by his second wife, Euphemia Ross, alone had an unquestioned right to succeed him, and that therefore David and Walter, the fourth and fifth sons mentioned in 1373, had a superior claim to the first three. The feud between the descendants of Elizabeth Mure and those of Euphemia Ross persisted for generations.

There are few medieval sovereigns about whom so little is

known, and of whom it is so difficult to form any clear picture, as Robert II and Robert III. The inevitable impression is that a famous dynasty, which was to produce so many men of remarkable ability, and so many men—and women—with fascinating and commanding personalities, made a somewhat pedestrian beginning. It is true that the sources, both record and narrative, are scanty, but it is also true that such contemporary evidence as exists has little to say of the character of the Kings and of any personal policy they may have pursued, and the inference must be that the first Stewarts to reign were men who did not much impress those who knew them. Admittedly, no attempt has yet been made to bring the resources of modern historical research to bear on Robert II and Robert III in the way that they have been brought to bear on Robert I and David II, but it is beyond the bounds of probability that even if this is done either of them will emerge as a man who did much positively to shape Scottish history.

Robert II was already very nearly fifty-five at the time of his accession, and he lived for another nineteen years, making him an uncommonly old man by the standards of the time. When he died he had attained a greater age than any other king who ever reigned in Scotland, and his years exceeded those of every other head of his house until the Old Pretender, who survived to the age of seventy-eight—but then he had never been burdened by the cares of kingship. Far and away the longer and more active part of Robert II's life was therefore lived before he became King, and from the age of thirteen to the age of fifty-four he was a subject of David II. His relations with that King may well have been prejudiced from the outset by the simple fact that Robert, as the son of David's elder half-sister, was David's nephew but was eight years older than his uncle. During David's long minority, and the troubles caused by the Edward Balliol episode, Robert the Steward held the position in the kingdom to which his place as heir presumptive entitled him. At the battle of Halidon Hill, when the Scots were routed by the English in 1333, Robert, though only seventeen, shared in the command,

and he was associated with the regency of the realm from 1335 onwards. In 1341, when he was twenty-five, he had to surrender his authority to the seventeen-year-old David on the latter's return from France. When David invaded England in 1346, on the expedition which resulted in his defeat and capture at Neville's Cross, the Steward was again one of the Scottish commanders, and he drew off the Scottish force—with, so it was said, indecent haste. It may well have been with some personal relief that he saw David a prisoner and himself elevated to the regency again for the eleven years of the King's captivity. After David's release in 1357, we next hear of the Steward as an associate of the Earls of Douglas and March in an unsuccessful rebellion against the King. What the motives of the conspirators were remains obscure. They are credited with a patriotic dislike of David's anglophile tendencies and a statesmanlike opposition to his squandering on his own pleasures money raised to pay his ransom. But personal grudges may well have been the main element in the episode. Besides, David's queen, Joanna, had died in 1362, leaving no children, and the Steward was necessarily much concerned lest the thirty-eight-year-old King might enter on a fruitful marriage. It was not until after the rebellion that David did in fact marry his second wife, Margaret Logie, but his intentions may already have been clear.

Robert II's career before his accession had been, to say the least, undistinguished, and his reign did nothing to add lustre to it. His more powerful subjects were not disposed to treat with much respect a man who was merely one of themselves who had been elevated to the throne through a fortunate marriage, and Robert's age brought increasing infirmity and incapacity. He was described in 1385 as having 'red bleared eyes, of the colour of sandal-wood, which clearly showed he was no valiant man, but one who would rather remain at home than march to the field'. By this time he was seventy, but his earlier experience of war at Halidon and Neville's Cross had not encouraged him to approve of military operations against England, and his more adventurous subjects found that when they did engage in expeditions across the Border they did well to conceal their plans from the King. It appears that as early as 1381 the King's eldest son, the Earl of Carrick, was associated in the government with his ageing father, and in 1384, because 'our lord the King, for certain causes, is not able himself to attend regularly and thoroughly in all things to the execution of the government and law of his kingdom', it was decided that Carrick should 'execute the common law . . . to all persons suffering grievance or wrong'. But in 1388 Carrick himself, after being lamed by a kick from a horse, became a chronic invalid, and then, on the ground of the 'infirmity' of Carrick, his younger brother, Robert, Earl of Fife, was appointed to do justice, maintain the laws and defend the kingdom.

In 1390, when Robert II died, it was his son and heir, whose 'infirmity' had been alluded to two years before, who was crowned at Scone. Thus, after nineteen years of the increasingly senile Robert II, Scotland was to have sixteen years of the infirm Robert III. This second Stewart King had been baptised John, but he was crowned as Robert to avoid the associations of a name which had been borne by a number of luckless monarchs: John of England had surrendered his kingdom to the pope; John Balliol had surrendered Scotland to Edward I; and John of France had been captured by the English at Poitiers. But the change of name did nothing to invigorate the new King, and he was noted more for a natural kindliness and a dislike of injustice than for the ability and energy which alone could have given order and equity to his subjects. More of the character which the name Robert was believed to denote was displayed by the King's brother, who had indeed been baptised Robert. This Robert, previously Earl of Fife and Menteith, is best known as the Duke of Albany, a title conferred on him in 1398. At the same time, the King's elder son, David, became Duke of Rothesay. His mother was Annabella Drummond, daughter of Sir John Drummond of Stobhall and niece of David II's queen, Margaret Logie; Robert III had married her about 1367 and Prince David had been born in 1378. Rothesay and Albany were the first two dukes created in

Scotland, and both titles were to have a long history. The style Duke of Rothesay has ever since been borne by the eldest son of the King of Scots and it is still—with the titles of Prince and High Steward of Scotland and Earl of Carrick—one of the titles of the Prince of Wales. The style Duke of Albany was almost invariably given to the King's second son as long as Scotland was a separate kingdom.

It was Robert, Duke of Albany, who dominated affairs during much of the nominal rule of his elder brother, though he did not have uninterrupted tenure of the office of lieutenant. In 1393 the King appears to have taken the administration into his own hands, and the results seem to have been disastrous. Disorder grew, and by 1398 it could be said that 'in those days there was no law in Scotland, but he who was strong oppressed the weak and the whole kingdom was one den of thieves. Homicides, ravagings and fire-raisings and all other evil deeds remained unpunished; and justice, outlawed, was in exile outwith the bounds of the kingdom.' The estates of the realm, meeting in a general council, blamed the unhappy King: 'the misgovernance of the realm and the default of the keeping of the common law should be imputed to the King and his officers'. And they added that if the King cared to excuse his faults he could produce his officers and accuse them before the council. The same meeting of the estates appointed David, Duke of Rothesay, the King's elder son, as lieutenant of the kingdom, but he was to act with the advice of a body of councillors among whom Albany's name stood first. Whether Rothesay or Albany was likely to make the better governor it is hard to say. The evidence is quite inadequate, but if Albany's reputation is one of self-seeking ambition, Rothesay's is one of pleasure-seeking folly. The King had already shown that he could not control one of his brothers, Alexander, who was known as 'the Wolf of Badenoch' and is best remembered because he burned Elgin Cathedral in 1390 and drove out the canons, who mildly complained of the 'misgovernment of the province of Moray'. And it is unlikely that Robert III could control his son either. It has been suggested that the one restraining influence on

Rothesay was that of his mother, but she died in 1401 and a crisis followed shortly thereafter.

Albany, it appears, persuaded the King to consent to the confinement of Rothesay at Falkland, and there he died in 1402. His death was so convenient for Albany that gossip was inevitable, and the council had to take steps to counteract it by declaring formally that the prince had 'departed this life through the divine dispensation and not otherwise'. It is true that the contemporary chronicler Wyntoun, who speaks well, if conventionally, of Rothesay as

> *honest, habill and avenand* . . . [comely]
> *Cunnand in to litterature,*
> *A seymly persone in stature,*

says without comment that he 'yielded his soul to his creator'. But the disquiet occasioned by Rothesay's death was never forgotten. Bower, writing about 1440, says that Rothesay died of dysentery 'or, as others would have it, of starvation', and fuller, picturesque details were supplied in the sixteenth century by Hector Boece, an author of many agreeable fictions, who had it that Albany imprisoned Rothesay 'in ane toure but [without] ony mete or drynk'. These details were worked by Sir Walter Scott into *The Fair Maid of Perth*, and it has been hard for anyone since Scott wrote to shake off the impression made by his account of the dramatic relationship between uncle and nephew. It is sometimes said that the Albany Aisle, in the church of St Giles at Edinburgh, which dates from the very early years of the fifteenth century, was built as an act of reparation or penance for Albany's guilt.

The fate of Rothesay may well have indicated that measures should be considered for the protection of his younger brother, James, but there is no evidence that immediate action was taken. In the spring of 1406, however, when the boy was in his twelfth year, arrangements were made for him to find safety in France. A strong armed force, under Sir David Fleming of Cumbernauld, a loyal servant and friend of the old King, conducted the prince to the fortress on the Bass Rock, where he was to await a ship on her way from Leith to France. There is no evidence that the death of Fleming, at the hands of Sir James Douglas of Balveny, who waylaid him on his way back from the coast, was an act stimulated by Albany, but it does show the disturbed state of the country. James spent over a month on the Bass, possibly because the equinoctial season discouraged shipping, but was at length put on board a vessel of Danzig ownership, carrying a cargo of wool and hides. The ship was attacked by English pirates off Flamborough Head, the crew were overpowered and the victors carried their prize before Henry IV, who rewarded them with the ship's cargo. It has been suggested that the wicked uncle, Albany, frustrated in one way when James was spirited out of Scotland, may have been a party to a deed which promised to put the Prince out of his way for a long time, if not for good. It can hardly be doubted that it was a sense of insecurity which had made King Robert retire to the castle of Rothesay in his ancestral island of Bute, and it was there that he died on 4 April 1406, possibly after learning of his son's capture.

2 Seal of Robert, I, 1306
From Anderson's 'Diplomata'

3

The Crown and its Rivals

Little prestige attached to Scottish kingship at the beginning of the fifteenth century, and it would have been hard to determine what pre-eminence, if any, the King possessed. After three baronial families—Balliol, Bruce and Stewart—had in turn been raised to the throne, there was no reason for confidence that the third house would prove more lasting than the first and second, and a succession repeatedly defined by statute might be altered by statute in favour of yet another dynasty. Even without any such change, authority might pass from the line possessed of the crown, for success in rule depended on personality, and the long government of Robert, Duke of Albany, first in the names of Robert II and Robert III and later, while James I was a prisoner in England, in his own name, showed that power and the royal title were not necessarily vested in the same person. Scotland was threatened with a line of 'mayors of the palace'.

The material resources of the crown, as well as its prestige, had to be weighed in the balance against those of the nobility, and when the comparison was made it was hard to see the King as even *primus inter pares* in relation to magnates with territorial possessions and ancient titles which gave them numbers of dependants among whom loyalty to the crown was secondary to loyalty to their lords. The tie between a feudal superior and his vassals was something that kings had to reckon with in all West European countries, but in Scotland the position of some at least of the magnates contained elements which owed nothing to feudalism and may indeed have been rooted in the conditions of pre-feudal society.

Before the fifteenth century an honorific earldom or lordship was as yet almost unthought of, and the territorial possessions of the holder of a title were what counted: an earldom or a lordship meant not merely a title, but wide powers and properties in one of the ancient regions which were not the creations of feudalism. The number of earls was small, each took his title from an historic region, and nearly all earldoms were of ancient, if not unknown, origin. Angus, Atholl, Buchan, Caithness, Fife, Lennox, Mar, Menteith, Ross, Strathearn and Sutherland were together roughly coextensive with the one-time kingdom of the Picts, and in some of those areas the earls were clearly the successors of the shadowy 'mormaers' who make an occasional appearance in sources for the period before 1153. Only two earldoms existed in the south—Carrick or southern Ayrshire, evidently created about 1200, and Dunbar or March in the south-east, which was a kind of offshoot of the English earldom of Northumbria. There were, besides, 'lords', who held lordships like Galloway, Annandale and Badenoch, which were hard to distinguish in either importance or character from the earldoms. It has been observed that, while a lordship could be created for one of the incoming Anglo-Normans, as the lordship of Annandale was for Bruce, their only chance of attaining an earldom was by marriage with an heiress. There was no question, it would seem, of creating a new earldom, at least in ancient Scotia north of the Forth, and this in itself would indicate that there were deep-rooted ties between an earl and his people.

During the fourteenth century there had been a considerable turnover of landed property, partly because of the forfeitures of magnates who had taken the English side in the wars and partly because of the failure of some of the native lines of earls. Thus, in the north-east, the Keiths (who became hereditary Marischals of the realm) and the Hays (who became hereditary Constables) rose on the ruin of the Comyns, who had been Earls of Buchan and had opposed the claims of Bruce to the throne. The family of Strathbogie, which had held the earldom of Atholl, was forfeited, and the possessions of the family were divided: in Strathbogie itself, the Gordons came in (from Berwickshire), and in Atholl, after some brief tenures by other families, Stewarts acquired the earldom. In the earldom of Angus, the Umfraville line was forfeited, and replaced by Stewarts, from whom the earldom passed to a branch of the Douglas family at the end of the fourteenth century. The lordship of Galloway, which had belonged to the Balliols, in the end went mainly to the Douglases. Comyn lands in Strathclyde went to the ancestor of the house of Hamilton. In Ayrshire the Boyds likewise rose to eminence as a result of forfeitures. The greatness of the Campbells in Argyll dates to some extent from the forfeiture of MacDougall of Lorne, who had been on the Comyn side. The families who thus came to the front under the Bruce dynasty—Gordons, Hamiltons and Campbells—were to rise still higher under the Stewarts.

With the accession of the Stewarts, and the need to provide for the numerous sons of Robert II, there was a fresh distribution of earldoms, following on some more forfeitures and failures of native lines. The earldoms of Fife and Menteith went to the King's eldest son, the earldoms of Buchan, Caithness, Strathearn and Atholl to others of his numerous progeny. These well-endowed sons may have looked like a phalanx round the throne, but in fact they represented a considerable potential weakness: not only were lands and revenues dissipated which might have been retained by the crown, but earls who were cadets of the royal house were apt to be peculiarly dangerous, as was to be shown by the careers of Robert, Earl of Fife and Menteith, and Walter, Earl of Atholl, in James I's reign. It was a stroke of good fortune for succeeding kings that neither Alexander, Earl of Buchan, nor David, Earl of Strathearn and Caithness, had sons to succeed them in their titles.

There was also in the fourteenth century one revival of an old earldom, that of Moray. There had in earlier times been kings and mormaers of Moray, but since the last of them was dispossessed by David I the province had presumably been in the hands of the crown. Then Robert I, as part of his policy of rewarding his supporters by somewhat lavish alienations of property, created an earldom of Moray for his nephew, Thomas Randolph. It was distinctly an earldom of the traditional, territorial type, for Randolph received very wide powers and his endowment included even the royal burghs within the bounds of Moray. He did not, however, found a lasting dynasty, for after Thomas and his two sons the male line of this family died out and the earldom passed to a Dunbar family who enjoyed far less prestige. Under David II we find the creation of some definitely new earldoms. In 1341 Sir Malcolm Fleming was elevated to an earldom of Wigtown, representing part of the old lordship of Galloway, and he was endowed, like Randolph in Moray, with a comprehensive jurisdiction and a royal burgh. In 1358 another completely new earldom, that of Douglas, was created, but this was essentially an integration into an earldom (which was probably second to none in importance) of the very extensive lands and jurisdictions previously conceded by Robert Bruce to Sir James Douglas, one of his lieutenants. It was more of an innovation when, in 1398, an earldom of Crawford made its appearance, at the same time as Scotland's first two dukedoms, Albany and Rothesay. Creations of new earldoms did not become common until the fifteenth century.

With the lands of the earls and other great subjects of the crown there went jurisdiction. Just as the King was nominally the ultimate owner of all land, so he was the fount of justice, and all justice nominally derived from him. But jurisdiction as well as land was alienated by the charters which created baronies and regalities, and a very substantial proportion of the administration of the law came into the hands of hereditary nobles, to the curtailment of the powers of the royal courts. A regality possessed a system of legal administration reproducing in miniature that of the kingdom, its courts had power to deal with all crimes except treason, the penalties exacted in its courts, in the shape of fines and forfeitures, accrued to the lord of regality and not to the crown. If a tenant of the regality was summoned before a royal justiciar, his landlord could demand that he be returned to be tried in the landlord's own court. It added to the judicial powers of the lords that many of them held the office of sheriff as a heritable office, so that the sheriff, though nominally a royal officer, was really a local magnate. All in all, the activities of baron courts, regality courts and hereditary sheriff courts were of far more account than the work of judges appointed by the King. Besides, many branches of law were administered not by secular courts at all but by the ecclesiastical courts, which had competence in executry and matrimonial cases and in proceedings for the fulfilment of contracts.

Lands and jurisdictions alike were granted, and defined, in charters from the crown, and charters defined, too, the feudal services which a lord could exact from his vassals and tenants. But the influence of a magnate depended on other factors which were not defined in charters and were not of the King's making. One of those was blood relationship. Kinship—'the kin'—was always an important element in Scottish life, and the practice was for men of the same family, or even of the same surname—whether or not they were demonstrably related by blood—to act together. If 'the kin' or 'the name' was one link which joined men together, the 'band' or 'bond' was another. A bond might join one magnate to another, almost in the manner of a treaty of political alliance, and it could constitute a great danger to the crown if great families were acting in concert. But, besides the bond between one magnate and another, there was another kind of bond, called a bond of manrent. This was a bond between a great man and some dependant, whereby the more lowly individual, in return for a promise of protection, undertook to be faithful to the other and support him in all his quarrels. Through the use of such bonds of manrent a magnate could greatly extend his following. The effects of such bonds were, indeed, not unlike those of the feudal ties between a superior and his vassals, but the bonds, unlike the charters defining the duties of tenants, were not associated with land tenure and were not necessarily hereditary. It should also be said that, apart from formal feudal obligations, and apart from the influence and even coercion which a landlord could bring to bear on his tenants, many men of lowly status often had a strong sense of a tradition of hereditary service to some noble house and considered themselves under moral obligations to follow the head of that house.

By those various means, a magnate created an extensive following, which may be thought of as a series of circles around him, though they were intersecting rather than concentric circles since one category of dependants overlapped with another. The Earl of Crawford, shall we say, had vassals to whom he had granted feudal charters of lands on condition of the rendering of certain services to him. He also held bonds of manrent by which a number of men of a social standing inferior to his own were obliged to take part with him in his quarrels and assist him in any action to further his interests. But the Earl's surname was Lindsay, and he could therefore rely on the support, in general, of Lindsays of high and low degree. Finally, both he and his more immediate dependants had their tenants and servants who were habituated to service on behalf of their landlords and masters. Out of this great complex of relationships there emerged the 'Crawford interest' or the 'Crawford following', which in the main acted as a unit.

Units of this kind played a conspicuous part in Scottish history in the fifteenth and sixteenth centuries. We shall see how 'the Livingstons' rose and fell together in the reign of James II and 'the Boyds' rose and fell together in that of James III. In the sixteenth century we shall see how Hamiltons and Douglases each established a temporary ascendancy and each in turn lost power and influence, and how the Hamilton following or the Douglas following was forfeited or was rehabilitated *en bloc.*

The Western Highlands and Islands presented problems of their own, but perhaps differing in degree rather than in kind from those of the rest of the country. The generality of the Highland clans did not at any time constitute a factor of major importance, though negatively their close-knit social structure and the configuration of the country which they inhabited made them obstacles to the assertion of royal power. The lordship of the Isles, however, represented a more serious challenge to the crown. There had been in earlier times a kingdom of the Isles, nominally subject to the Norwegian crown in the period before the Hebrides were ceded to Scotland in 1266, and in the fourteenth century a branch of the MacDonald family adopted the style of Lords of the Isles and was long a focal point for separatist ambitions. The lordship itself seems to have included some territories on the west mainland, and from early in the fifteenth century it was, in consequence of a fortunate marriage, held in conjunction with the earldom of Ross, so that a single magnate controlled great tracts of the north and west mainland as well as the Western Isles. It would have been too much to expect anything like consistent loyalty to the Scottish crown from people who had become its subjects so recently as 1266, and the allegiance of the Lords of the Isles to the King of Scots was at best intermittent. Thus, Angus MacDonald supported Robert Bruce, and, like Randolph and Douglas, was rewarded from the lands of chiefs who had opposed Bruce; but John, son of Angus, joined Edward Balliol against David II, and later members of the family were active on the side of the English Kings Edward IV and Henry VIII. None of the earlier Stewart rulers seems to have gained anything like the confidence and support of his western subjects. So far as the rank and file of the Highlanders were concerned, it seems to have been a matter of indifference whether they were led out on behalf of Scottish or English kings.

The problem of government and of upholding the ruling house against powerful combinations, whether of Lowlanders or Highlanders, was made the more difficult by the precarious nature of the royal succession. At the best, it very often happened that only the King's own life stood between some noble family and a royal inheritance to which it had good right by blood and even by statute. Thus, two Dukes of Albany and an Earl of

Atholl were successively heirs presumptive to James I, two Dukes of Albany were heirs presumptive to James III, James IV and James V, an Earl of Arran was heir presumptive to Mary. But beyond the rights of heirs presumptive, there were, for half a century and more, the claims of Robert II's descendants by his second and unquestionably legal marriage. Those claims were more dangerous than those of heirs presumptive, for they were claims not to succeed, but to supplant, the senior line. The descendants in the male line of that marriage were extinguished in 1437, but a succession through a female continued, and in this succession there stood the powerful house of Douglas. No doubt statute was against their claims through a female, but what one statute had done another could undo.

It is easy to analyse and demonstrate the weakness of the crown in material resources as well as in prestige. The paucity of its landed possessions in the reigns of the first Stewarts is startling, for it would appear that before its extensive acquisitions in the course of the fifteenth century it can have had little save the patrimony of the Bruces and the Stewarts in Carrick, Renfrew and Bute. Nor did the crown have very substantial alternative sources of revenue to compensate for its poverty in land. Taxation was so far from being as yet a normal instrument of government that a foreign observer at the end of the fifteenth century, although he was anxious to magnify the Scottish King's resources, does not even mention it. Some of the regular sources of revenue were almost static. The ferms paid by the royal burghs were by this time a negligible item even in gross, they were so heavily burdened by assignations and pensions that hardly anything came to the crown, and they were not capable of any appreciable increase, since most important burghs, if not all, paid a sum fixed in perpetuity. The yield of the customs, again, was not likely to rise except as trade increased. The feudal casualties of ward, relief, nonentry and marriage which fell to the crown were often given away either gratis or for small compositions. The proceeds from fines in local courts were negligible, because only small compositions were made over, though the circuits or justice ayres held intermittently for criminal cases could produce worthwhile sums.

Lacking financial resources from which substantial military or police forces could have been maintained, the crown was without the executive agents who could have preserved law and order and put into effect the decisions of the central government. Sometimes the only action the crown could take against disorder was to play on the rivalries and feuds of the leading families and endow one magnate with authority to levy war against another. This was little better than setting a thief to catch a thief, and it was apt to create as many problems in the future as it solved at the time. In normal times there was not much, throughout the country, to impress on anyone's consciousness an awareness of the authority of the central government or even of the existence of a central government at all. The only officials to be seen permanently in the localities were local magnates, in the shape of barons and lords of regalities, or their officers, and even when local magnates were disguised as sheriffs it was not at once obvious that they represented delegated royal authority. Officers did occasionally come directly from the central government on one errand or another, but there was so little habit of obedience to them that it was their common fate to be 'deforced' or violently obstructed in the discharge of their duties. There were no 'government buildings' throughout the country save the royal castles, and even these were in the custody of local magnates, thinly disguised now as keepers or captains.

What was true of the financial system and the legal system was true also of the parliamentary system, for there again it was land that mattered and it was the great men who carried sway. It was land that mattered, because it was, in a sense, land that was represented in parliament, rather than the people. Nearly all who were there held land, and held it of the King. The nobles, as tenants-in-chief of the crown, were of course entitled to attend in person, and most of the clergy who were present, the bishops and abbots, were also great landowners. There were burgess representatives from the early fourteenth century onwards, but they came mainly from the royal burghs, where the land was held of the crown, and even among the forty or so royal burghs which existed by 1500 by no means all were regularly represented in parliament; sometimes a mere handful were represented. An attempt was made by James I, in 1428, to strengthen the middle-class element in parliament by providing for the election of shire commissioners who would represent the lesser tenants of the crown, but it proved abortive, and parliament remained predominantly drawn from the higher social levels until the late sixteenth century. The three estates, the nobles, prelates and burgesses, met and deliberated in one chamber, and, in the absence of shire representation, there could be no development of any effective counter to the voice of the magnates, no development like the English House of Commons.

One may say briefly that landholding, government and society were all alike feudal, in that power and influence went with land and administration was in the hands of the great landholders. One might say again, with equal truth, that the crown, unable to dominate the great feudatories either by superior wealth or by force, could maintain the government only by coming to terms with some of them.

On the other hand, it is also plain that in its contest with its rivals the crown had certain assets, though they were mainly of an intangible kind. For one thing, the monarchy derived great strength from the fact that it was regarded as a desirable and useful institution which was, for entirely practical reasons, little short of a necessity in the life of the nation. The whole legal system was conducted in the King's name, so that the crown was an essential element, for which no alternative had yet been so much as considered, in that system. Equally, in a country where landholding was wholly feudalised, the crown was indispensable in the system of land tenure and conveyancing. The crown was also the source of patronage, in the widest sense of that term. It could grant lands, pensions and the feudal casualties which accrued to it, it could also make appointments to offices which conferred both power and profit. This meant that the crown was the dispenser of things that ambitious men wanted and this gave it enormous potential influence. It is not surprising that an opposition never wanted to abolish the monarchy, or perhaps even to reduce its authority: the opposition wanted to control the crown and enjoy what the crown could bestow, in lands and offices and revenues, but the aim never seems to have been any alteration in the constitution. It may have been partly for this reason that any opposition was, as a rule, vague in its objectives and sometimes irresolute in action—a fact which was, though negatively, a further asset to the crown. Our evidence is scanty, but so far as it goes it rather indicates that any baronial opposition was concerned mainly to check the growth of the power of the crown over their properties and franchises.

A strong and active king, exercising in person the powers, privileges and patronage attached to his office, could make his rule effective. He could himself direct the legal system which was carried on in his name; he could control the distribution of land and the jurisdiction which went with land; and he could use his patronage to buy support and reward his faithful servants. A vigorous king could even do much to extend royal justice, partly by providing for the regular holding of justice ayres for criminal cases and partly by arranging for the hearing of civil cases by permanent 'sessions' of judges appointed by either parliament or council. While attempts to curb the granting of regalities were not very successful, and the central as well as the local courts were still, throughout the fifteenth century, in the hands of amateur part-time judges, the period from James I to James IV on the whole showed an increase of royal justice. There was one judicial process in particular which was a valuable weapon in the hands of a king who could use it wisely, and that was the sentence of forfeiture, which could be passed only by parliament and usually only for treason against the King's person. This was the ultimate sanction against unruly subjects, and their fear of it may explain the reluctance of even the most ambitious nobles to face the King in the field; time and again a rebellion petered out, the rebel army melted away, when the sovereign personally took command of the loyal forces. Forfeitures involved the annexation of estates to the crown and its consequent enrichment, but there was also the opportunity to grant the estates out afresh. From time to time, notably in 1455, attempts were made to ensure that the core of the crown's patrimony in land and jurisdiction would not be alienated, but the intention declared in the Act of Annexation of 1455 was not strictly fulfilled, and although there were many later acts of revocation and acts of annexation they were not strictly fulfilled either. Yet some progress was made: in the reign of each king from James I to James V earldoms and lordships were forfeited to the crown, they were not all re-granted, and over the period the landed wealth of the kings did increase, until they were unquestionably superior in resources to even the greatest of the nobles. Probably nothing did more to secure the monarchy than the policy which the kings on the whole pursued, of acquiring great lordships and earldoms and keeping them or some of them in their own hands. James I acquired Fife, Strathearn and Mar, James II the Douglas properties, James III Orkney and Shetland and part of the lordship of the Isles, James IV the remainder of that lordship and James V the properties of the Earl of Angus.

While even the impersonal crown was an important unifying factor in the country, the personal king could and often did increase his importance in this respect if he moved around the country to show his face to his people. Most of the kings made frequent, almost regular, circuits in central Scotland, residing for periods at Perth, Stirling, Linlithgow, Edinburgh and Falkland. There were two practical reasons for such movements: when sanitation was rudimentary, even the most hardened thought it desirable to move quarters from time to time in order to allow a period of cleansing; and when transport was primitive it was easier to move the king and his court to centres where they could consume the foodstuffs which crown tenants were obliged to render than to convey the foodstuffs to a capital. But, over and above the customary circuit of central Scotland, James I and James II made occasional visits further afield which had political objectives, and when James III, in his minority, was conducted on a tour in the north, the reason must have been political. Later, James IV's unresting movements took him to places ranging from Whithorn in the south to Tain in the north and from Aberdeen in the east to the Sound of Mull and some of the Inner Hebrides in the west. James V outdid his father by embarking on a cruise to the Northern and Western Isles and visiting some places which never saw royalty again until the present reign. The royal progresses went hand in hand with an increase in royal wealth and an extension of royal justice, and the effects must have been to impress on the subjects the significance and reality of the kingship in a way that would have been unthinkable in the days of Robert II and Robert III.

It is impossible to determine how far, if at all, the kings aimed at making a bid for the support of the middle and lower classes against the nobility. On the whole, they seem rather to have thought in terms of using the existing social structure to the extent that they endeavoured to win to their side a proportion of the nobles (who, of course, brought with them their following). It is true that in each reign there was a good deal of legislation which benefited all classes in the nation, and some which was aimed specifically at benefiting the lower classes. Probably the most significant acts of this nature were those designed in one way and another to give tenants greater security in their holdings and liberate them from entire dependence on the will, or the whim, of their landlords. One of James I's statutes, for example, forbade prelates and barons, during the period of one year, to remove any tenants unless the lands were going to be taken into the landlord's own hands. This was a somewhat feeble measure, but it showed an awareness that insecurity of tenure was a grievance. In James II's reign, an act of 1449 ordained that, when the ownership of lands changed, the tenants should not be liable to eviction unless their leases had expired, but should continue to hold their farms at the old rents. Later in the same reign, parliament urged that crown lands should be granted out not in lease but in 'feu'—that is, in heritable tenure in return for a duty fixed in perpetuity

—and that other proprietors should be encouraged to follow the royal example. Under James III, in 1469, an act ordained that tenants were not to be responsible for the debts of their landlords, and under James IV it was enacted that when an estate changed hands the tenants were to sit until the following Whitsunday term and were not to be arbitrarily evicted. All such acts seem to be clearly aimed at improving the lot of tenants, and certainly cannot be viewed as in the interests of selfish landlords. There were also, reign by reign, measures aimed at encouraging, or even compelling, better husbandry and fuller use of the arable land, and there were sometimes acts for the conservation of trees and for 'improvements' such as plantations, orchards, parks and hedges. The interests of subjects other than tenant-farmers were served by grants of privileges to burghs, by proposals for uniform standards of weights and measures and by acts against incompetent or careless smiths and against ferrymen who overcharged their passengers.

It is not easy to assess the significance of all this well-intentioned legislation and to determine how far, if at all, an altruistic desire for the welfare of the generality of the king's subjects lay behind it. In so far as the aim was to increase the prosperity and productivity of the country, the motives may not have been disinterested, for any increase of wealth in the country would indirectly increase the revenue and resources of the crown. In the same context may be placed some of the legislation against certain recreations which interfered both with military training and with productive labour: statutes of James I, James II and James IV forbade the playing of football, and James II's prohibition extended to golf as well. Such acts can hardly have been popular, but possibly those kings had some austere and industrious subjects who heartily approved of a ban on unprofitable occupations and thought that their fellows would do better to be engaged in agriculture or crafts. So far as the legislation in favour of 'the poor tenants' on the land is concerned, it has to be kept in mind that some concept of social justice lay behind the reciprocal relationship between lord and man, for the latter expected protection in return for his services, and there is no reason to believe that the policy of the crown alone was necessarily responsible for those measures or that they were believed to be contrary to the wider interests of the more far-seeing landlords.

We cannot, therefore, conclude that the kings were deliberately playing for the support of the middle and lower classes. Possibly the most important means by which they might win such support was by their actions on their progresses, when they could be freely approached by men of every class and had every opportunity to ingratiate themselves. It has been said with truth that as James IV moved around the country his subjects learned to recognise and admire his sympathy, generosity and strong sense of justice. But no appeal that any king could make, whether by legislation, attention to suitors or acts of personal kindness, was likely effectively to counter the sway of the magnates over the mass of their dependants.

All in all, there were certain potentialities in the kingship which provided opportunities for a vigorous king to extend his authority. But the periods of rule by energetic monarchs were separated from each other by minorities or by periods of rule by weak kings. During such intervals, the powers, privileges and patronage of kingship, far from being used to strengthen the central government, were prizes to be competed for by individuals or factions—and of minorities and the rule of weak kings Scotland had more than its share. This was, of course, one consequence of strict adherence to hereditary succession within the Stewart line. Hereditary succession had its obvious advantages, in obviating disputes about the crown; but it had the disadvantage that it involved the acceptance as kings of minors and of men otherwise unfit for the office. In the whole period between the death of Robert I and the union of the crowns in 1603 the Scottish kingship was strong in the person of the king for a total of less than 100 years out of nearly 300: for two-thirds of the time Scotland did not have a king ruling effectively. After the minority and captivity of David II came the senility of Robert II, the infirmity of Robert III and then the captivity of James I. The persistent trouble, however, was minorities. Between the death of Robert III and the union of the crowns there were no less than six minorities—in seven reigns; every king from James I to James VI, with the solitary exception of James IV, succeeded as a child, three of them as mere infants. In the minority there is a regent, or a governor, who can secure his position only by bribing possible rivals with grants of crown lands and crown revenues, and if his position is not unchallenged, there are tumults between factions striving for control of the young king's person. Each minority was therefore marked by dilapidation of the resources of the crown and by kaleidoscopic changes in the government as one family or another attained a temporary ascendancy.

The numerous minorities did not result in consistent law and practice defining either the age of majority or the arrangements for regencies. It may seem curious that constant experience did not produce consistency, and the opportunism which clearly prevailed is itself significant of the predominance of individual and family interests rather than policy. In private law, a boy was in a state of pupillarity, and his affairs in the care of a tutor, until he reached the age of fourteen, a girl until she was twelve, and thereafter the child's affairs were managed by curators (whom he or she could now choose) until the age of twenty-one. It was understood that the tutor, who managed the affairs of the pupil, would normally be the heir presumptive, whose interest was to conserve the property of the minor, but that the person of the pupil should be in the hands of an individual other than the tutor (whose interest in the succession was felt to make him unsuited to have custody of the pupil's person). These rules were only partially applied in royal minorities. When an infant succeeded to the throne, his or her person was necessarily in the care of the queen mother at least for a time, but the queen mother usually had some voice in affairs as well, whether or not the new sovereign was an infant. Experience in the minorities of James II and James III showed that, after the queen mother ceased to have the custody of her child, the young King's person was apt to be seized by ambitious barons, and it seems later to have become the practice to commit the care of the King's person to someone who commanded general respect for his integrity and neutrality. For reasons which are not apparent, the Lords Erskine, later Earls of Mar, came to have an hereditary right to the custody of princes. The fifth Lord Erskine appears as one of the three lords who had the custody of the young James V in 1517, and in 1522 he seems to have had sole charge of the King. In 1540, when James V set out on his cruise to the Isles, he committed the care of his infant son and heir to Lord Erskine. Mary, Queen of Scots, was under the charge of Lord Erskine, as well as her mother, in the early years of her life. When Mary was succeeded by her one-year-old son, that Prince was placed in charge of the sixth Lord Erskine (who had become Earl of Mar in 1562) and, after Mar's death in 1572, the keeping of the King passed to Mar's brother. James VI continued the tradition by making the Earl of Mar responsible for the care of Prince Henry, his eldest son and heir. The Erskine family also had the keepership of Stirling Castle, where youthful princes were often brought up, but whether their tenure of this office was the cause or the consequence of their having the custody of royal children is not clear.

If the rule about the custody of the royal person was thus crystallising, the rule that the tutor should be the heir apparent was hardly capable of regular observance owing to the precarious state of the succession. When James II became King, the male lines on whom the crown had been entailed in 1373 were all extinct, so that there was no acknowledged heir presumptive, and the heirs presumptive to James III and James IV were their own younger brothers. Only on the accession of James V do we find an indubitable heir presumptive of mature years, in the person of John, Duke of Albany, and it was he who was accepted as governor. When Mary succeeded, it was again the heir presumptive, James, Earl of Arran, who became tutor and governor. In the minority of James VI, when there was again uncertainty about the heir presumptive, the first two regents were the Earl of Moray, Queen Mary's illegitimate half-brother, and the Earl of Lennox, the King's nearest kinsman on his father's side.

There was even more uncertainty about the age at which minority ended. James II and James III each began to take an active part in directing affairs at about the age of eighteen, and nothing of any significance had happened when they were fourteen. It is, however, perhaps worth noting that James III had been conducted on a progress in the north when he was twelve and that a declaration which he made in parliament when he was fifteen indicates that he was by that time considered capable of selecting his own advisers. James IV was just over fifteen when he succeeded, and there seems to have been no question of a regency. James V was formally 'erected' as King when he was just over twelve, but, two years later, there was a formal declaration that, as he had come to the age of fourteen, the royal authority was in his hands. The age at which he first became personally active in affairs was, however, sixteen. In Mary's case it was clearly held that when she reached the age of twelve she was capable of disposing of the regency; her personal rule may be dated from her mother's death (when she was in her eighteenth year) or from her return to Scotland (when she was in her nineteenth year). James VI was nominally vested with authority about three months before he was twelve, and the precise point at which he emerged from tutelage and became personally responsible for the direction of affairs is hard to determine. The one thing that emerges is that the normal age of majority—twenty-one—has no relationship to the age at which kings assumed authority. It would rather appear that at any point after his fourteenth birthday a boy could assert himself and take over the government, but the age of twelve was evidently thought to have some significance for males as well as for females.

On becoming the effective head of the government, at whatever age, a King was apt to deal firmly—sometimes brutally—with those who had governed during his minority, or who threatened his supremacy. But this did not mean that he was launching an unprovoked attack on 'the nobility' as a whole. And if it is thus wrong to generalise about 'the nobility' as victims of royal aggression, it is equally wrong to see them as a cohesive political group antagonistic to the crown. On the contrary, most kings could count on, or were able to gain, the support of a significant number of nobles. At the same time the fact remains that reign by reign there were magnates who were prepared not only to rebel, but to renounce their allegiance, to form treasonable leagues with England, to deny the right of the reigning monarch to the title of King of Scots; and to present the nobles as innocent victims of royal aggrandisement is to ignore the fate of James III at the hands of a baronial faction. Royal aggrandisement there certainly was, but before a King could consolidate his position he might be cut off by a sudden death while still in his prime—James II and James V were only thirty, James III was thirty-six and James IV was forty. Each minority meant a set-back for the monarchy, and some of the ground gained by one King was apt to be lost before his successor came of age. There was, if not a 'mournful procession of the five Jameses',* at any rate a melancholy repetition of the same pattern.

*F. W. Maitland, in *Cambridge Modern History*, ii, 551

3 The Palace and Abbey of Dunfermline
From John Slezer, 'Theatrum Scotiae'

4

An Angry Man in a Hurry: James I, 1406-37

James, the second son of Robert III and his Queen to survive infancy, was born towards the end of July 1394. If his birthday was the twenty-fifth of the month, the festival of St James the Great, this would explain why he was baptised with a name which had previously been borne by only one head of the Stewart family—his great-great-grandfather—but which was from this point to be transmitted through the house for nine generations. The Prince did not succeed to the dukedom of Rothesay after the death of his elder brother in 1402, but he was created Earl of Carrick in December 1404.

When James was captured on his way to France, in 1406, Henry IV of England is alleged to have said that there was no need for the boy to go to the continent for lessons in French, as he himself could teach that language. It can hardly be doubted that James in fact already knew French, for both his mother and his brother corresponded in that tongue, but Henry's joke had its significance, for the English King was a cultured and educated man and the schooling of his prisoner was not neglected. Possibly education of a formal kind was welcome to relieve the tedium of a captivity which lasted for eighteen years, from the age of twelve to the age of thirty, but it appears that James had a genuine love of scholarship as well as the ability to profit from his instructors. Besides, although he was at first lodged in the Tower of London, and returned there from time to time over the years, during much of his captivity he shared the life of Henry's court as it moved about the country. He therefore became versed in all the accomplishments and exercises fashionable among men of high birth, and his later career suggests that he also took an intelligent interest in learning how the government of England was conducted under the House of Lancaster.

In June 1406, two months after James's capture and Robert III's death, a general council of the Scottish estates recognised James as King and authorised the Duke of Albany to continue as Governor. Since the King was absent and uncrowned, it may be unsound to see anything sinister in the fact that Albany's acts now ran in his own name, as Governor, and not in that of King James; but it has often been remarked that Albany allowed James to remain in captivity although he succeeded in 1415 in securing the release of his own son, Murdoch, who had been taken prisoner by the English in 1402. It can hardly be doubted that Albany, who had exercised the office of Governor intermittently since Robert II was declared infirm in 1384, aimed at the perpetuation of the office in his own family, and when he died in 1420, at the age of eighty, he was in fact succeeded by Murdoch, who, like his father, ruled in his own name. It seems that the elder Albany, in his anxiety to make his rule acceptable, refrained from exercising authority wherever it might be resented; he allowed far too much latitude to the magnates, and he did nothing to discourage the spoliation of the crown's revenues. He delegated the oversight of northern and southern Scotland to the two most powerful nobles, the Earl of Mar and the Earl of Douglas. It may, however, be less than fair to reproach Albany with the fact that he declared that while he was governor no tax should be levied 'lest the poor curse him who introduced such an abuse', for this may indicate no more than the mild kindliness which is counted a virtue in his brother, Robert III. A near contemporary remarked that Albany 'sought the blessings of the common people beyond measure', but he had in truth more to gain from the blessings of the nobles than from those of the common people, and he could most easily gain the nobles' acquiescence in his rule by permitting them to seize crown property or raid the customs. All in all, effective central government was in danger of lapsing even under the elder Albany. It was worse when Duke Murdoch succeeded, for he lacked his father's ability, and the weakness of his rule may have arisen from incapacity rather than from deliberate policy. Douglas continued to rule in the south, though now perhaps in defiance of Murdoch rather than as his lieutenant. Murdoch's own sons were beyond any control by their father, and pursued lawlessness with impunity.

James seems to have become active in attempts to achieve his freedom in 1412, when he was eighteen. Besides writing letters which amounted to reproaching Albany for his reluctance to take any effective action towards his King's release, James may at this time have made a bid for support among some leading Scots. Not many examples are known of his exercise of anything resembling regal powers during his captivity, but two of them belong to this period. On 30 November 1412, at Croydon, he issued letters in favour of Sir William Douglas of Drumlanrig and his brother Archibald confirming them in their lands of Drumlanrig, Hawick, Selkirk and Cavers. The documents were issued 'under the signet usit in selyng of oure letters', but contained undertakings that formal ratifications would pass the great seal 'in tyme to come'. The actual manuscripts are said to be 'wrate with our propre hand', and are the earliest specimens which have survived of the penmanship of any King of Scots. It is not impossible that some earlier Kings could write, but it is not flattering to Scots, who boast of the merits of their country's educational system, that the first of their kings whose handwriting has come down to us was one who had the advantage of schooling in England. If those documents in favour of the Douglases were an effort to gain support for the King's return, they were fruitless at the time, but it is likely that James kept in touch with a family which was all-powerful in the south of Scotland and which in the end played a part in bringing about his release.

Throughout most of his captivity, James can hardly have been considered by his gaolers to have been of much political importance. Only should a Scottish government be prepared to concede terms favourable to England in return for his release, or should it be desirable to set up a competitor against a Scottish government which was militantly anti-English, would James become significant. His value suddenly increased owing to the turn which international events took in 1419. Henry V had been at war with France for several years, he had won his great victory of Agincourt in 1415, and he was in a fair way to realising that dream of medieval English monarchs, the conquest of France. But in 1419 the hard-pressed French received the assistance of some 6,000 or 7,000 Scots, under the Earl of Buchan, son of the elder Albany, and the newcomers, by their victory at Baugé in March 1421, broke the spell of English invincibility and did much to stimulate the French into a renewed resistance which was ultimately successful. In an attempt to neutralise the Scottish force, James was taken to France in 1420 and again in 1421, so that the Scots in France could be accused of fighting against their lawful sovereign.

In 1420 James was in England, for the coronation of Henry's French Queen, Catharine, at Westminster, and shortly afterwards he was knighted at Windsor. While he was thus becoming of more consequence in England, changes favourable to his hopes were taking place in Scotland. As the incompetence of Duke Murdoch, the Governor, became patent, there was an increasing desire for the King's return on the part of all who suffered from misrule, and a lead was given by the Earl of Douglas to those who were prepared to work for James's release. The death of Henry V in 1422, resulting in confused counsels in England during the minority of the infant Henry VI, improved James's prospects, and it was clear by the summer of 1423 that his return to his kingdom was a real possibility. From the English point of view, James's restoration would at least bring about the downfall of a Governor who had been encouraging Scottish intervention in France.

It was at this stage that there occurred the best known episode in James's captivity—the romance which he himself recounted in his poem *The Kingis Quair*. In it he relates that he was lying awake at midnight in his prison chamber and, being unable to sleep, read a portion of a work of Boethius. Shutting the book, he meditates on the reverses of fortune until he hears the bell ring for mattins. He determines to write a poem, and begins it with an account of his state of doubt, misery and uncertainty. After invoking the muses, he gives an account of the chief events of his youth, his departure from home, his capture at sea and his imprisonment. To divert his thoughts, he walks to the window. This is the turning point of his life, for he hears in the garden below the cheerful song of the nightingale and presently sees a lady with whom he falls in love at first sight:

And therewith kest I doun myn eye ageyne,
Quhare as I saw, walking under the toure,
Full secretly new cummyn hir to pleyne,
The fairest or the freschest yonge floure
That ever I sawe, me thoght, before that houre,
For quhich sodayn abate, anon astert
The blude of all my body to my hert.

The poem continues through a total of 197 stanzas of seven lines each, relating invocations of classical goddesses, with whose encouragement he is in the end successful in his suit.

The lady of the poem, or at any rate the lady of James's choice, was Joan Beaufort, daughter of the Earl of Somerset; as her father was a brother of Henry IV, she was a cousin of Henry V. 'Romance', it has been remarked, 'found the very match which policy would have dictated.'* It certainly appears that the projected marriage of James to Joan brought him more liberty and improved his prospects of release. His falling in love with her, whether or not it occurred precisely as he relates in his

*John Hill Burton, *History of Scotland*, ii, 397

poem, may with some confidence be dated at Windsor in May 1423, and from that point events moved rapidly.

In December, by the Treaty of London, it was agreed that James should be released in return for a payment of £40,000 in six annual instalments. Henry IV's joke about teaching him French had not been forgotten, and the payment was alleged to be due for the cost of his maintenance and education in England; but, while the annual expense of keeping James was now assessed at 2,000 merks, the highest sum ever known to have been granted to his keeper for his maintenance in a single year was only about half that sum, £700. The payment of £40,000 was, in fact, a ransom, and it was laid down that twenty-one named Scots of high birth should become hostages in England until full payment was made. One significant clause in the treaty provided that, while Scottish soldiers who had already left for France were not to be recalled, there were to be no further reinforcements. Two months after the treaty, on 13 February 1424, James and Joan were married in the church of St Mary Overy (now Southwark Cathedral). One-sixth of the ransom (10,000 merks) was remitted as a dowry for the bride. The King and Queen returned to Scotland in April, to be crowned at Scone on 2 May.

Coming to the throne as he did, after a succession of rulers who had been either incompetent by nature or mild by policy, James I had to labour to revive the royal authority by recovering the crown's resources and setting up machinery for the enforcement of law and order. But the restoration of effective administration would have been in vain, or would even have been impossible, unless he had first destroyed those who were likely to challenge his authority. The crown's rivals were, of course, to be found among the leading nobles, and chief among them were the members of the house of Albany. In May 1424, the very month of the coronation, James arrested Sir Walter Stewart, the eldest surviving son of Duke Murdoch. Sir Walter had been keeper of the fortress of Dumbarton, commanding a port which was second to none as a means of ingress to and egress from the centre of the kingdom and which was also a regular channel of communication with France. We know that he had made inroads on the customs which exceeded the fees to which he was entitled; we know that he planned to marry an heiress who would bring him the earldom of Mar to add to those of Fife and Menteith which he could expect to inherit from his father; and we know that he was actively fostering the French connection. But, although Sir Walter's doings were contrary to the King's policy, they were not crimes. Possibly the most cogent reason and justification for his arrest was that it would stop the sending of reinforcements to France and so prevent a violation of the Treaty of London.

Later in the same year, the old Earl of Lennox, father-in-law of Duke Murdoch, was imprisoned, and in 1425 Murdoch himself, with his wife and his youngest son, Alexander, was arrested. Meantime, James, another son of Murdoch, raised a revolt in the Lennox area, and he burned the town of Dumbarton. If the arrested members of the Albany family had had any chance of acquittal and release, this rebellion sealed their fate. Murdoch, his father-in-law and his sons Walter and Alexander were all executed, and Murdoch's earldoms of Fife and Menteith, as well as that of Lennox, were annexed to the crown. James, the son of Murdoch who had led the rebellion, fled to Ireland, and his followers, who had been holding out in the castle of Inchmurrin, on Loch Lomond, surrendered. What the criminal charges against Murdoch and his kinsmen had been is not known, and consequently it is impossible to assess the justification in law, if any, for their execution. But there was plainly some justification in policy, for the family was bound to be a focus of discontent with the King's administration. It has, however, been suggested that James was influenced against the Albany line by the Earl of Atholl, who stood next to them in the statutory succession and for whom the King had evidently a preference: 'While it is thus impossible to be sure about the justice of the punishment, it seems that political necessity combined with the cupidity of James and the malevolence of Atholl to require the removal of a family disposed to resist the royal policy of law and order, and able from its wealth, its rank and the prestige of recent office to lead an opposition which might have overthrown the King himself. The events of Dumbarton and Inchmurrin prove it no idle dread that Albany might have returned to rule, not as Governor but as King, when James should have been killed after one short year of active monarchy. The danger was now averted; the King had proved that high rank was no defence for lawlessness; the crown was enriched by the revenues of Fife, Menteith and Lennox.'*

Possibly those few months after the return of James I were the most critical point in the whole century for the ruling house, because there was never again such a real danger that it would be superseded. Yet those who were next in the royal succession after the Albanys were in a sense more dangerous, because, while the Albanys were in law only heirs presumptive to James, the next lines, descended from the second, and unquestionably lawful, marriage of Robert II, could claim a right superior to that of James. David, Earl of Strathearn, the elder son of Robert II by Euphemia Ross, had died in the 1380s, leaving only a daughter, Euphemia, who married Sir Patrick Graham and died about 1434. Her son, Malise Graham, was the senior male representative of the Euphemia Ross line, and had expected to succeed to his grandfather's earldom of Strathearn. In 1427 James denied it to him, on the ground that it was a male fief, which his mother had had no right to transmit: the lesson intended to be conveyed was that the crown also was restricted to the male line and that Malise did not inherit his grandfather's right in the royal succession. The same thought seems to have been in the mind of Charles I two centuries later, when he refused to allow the descendant of Malise to make good his claim to the earldom of Strathearn, with its hint of a right to the crown. Malise was compensated with the poorer earldom of Menteith, and was sent to England as one of the hostages for the King's unpaid ransom. Next to the Strathearn family stood Walter, Earl of Atholl, youngest son of Robert II. James seems to have attempted, with temporary success, to conciliate him, and by giving him the earldom of Strathearn tacitly admitted his place in the royal succession.

*E. W. M. Balfour-Melville, *James I, King of Scots*, 125

THE DOUGLASES AND THE ROYAL SUCCESSION

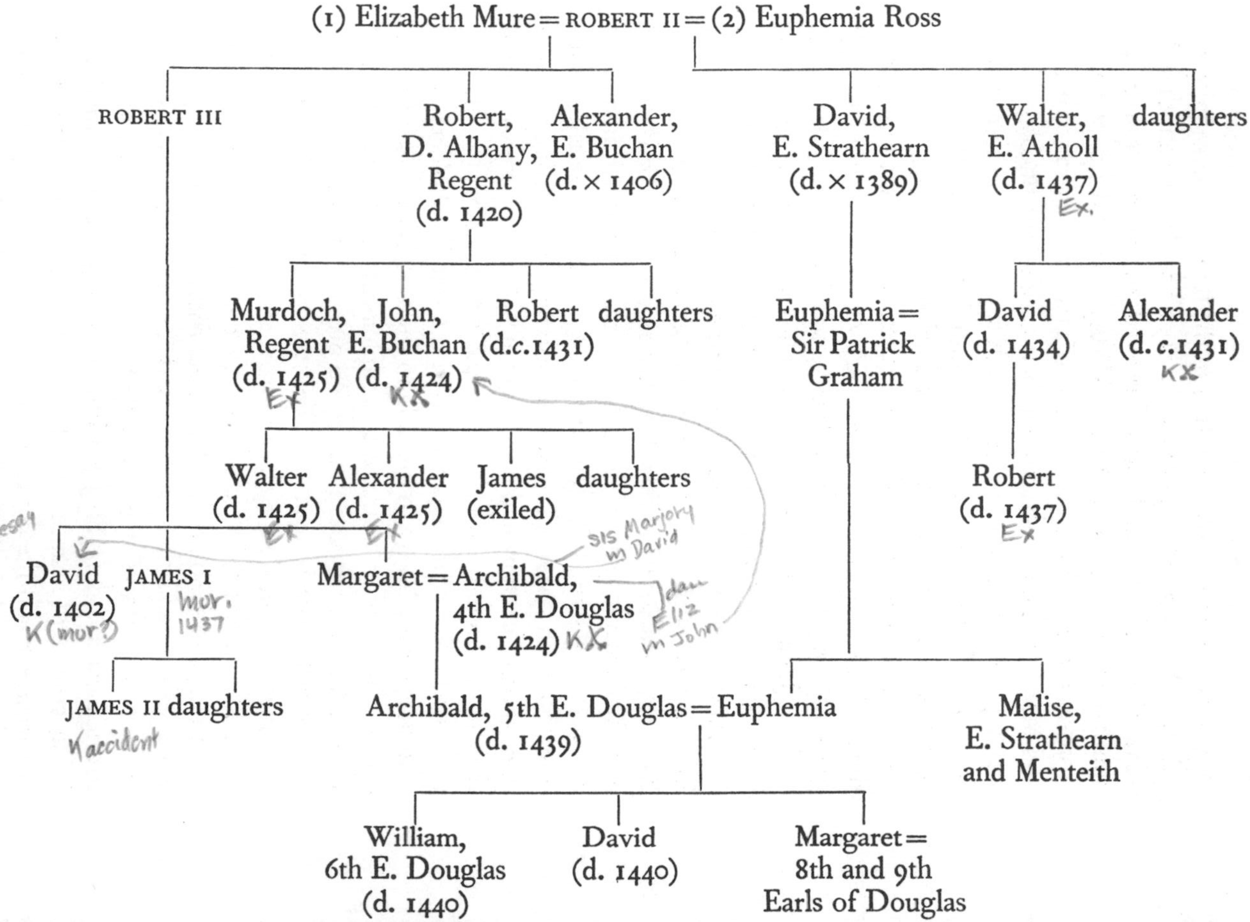

It was not only nobles standing in the line of succession to the throne who suffered at James's hands at one time or another. In 1434 the Earl of March was deprived of his earldom in the south-east, on the ground that Albany had had no power to restore it after the forfeiture of the earl's father a generation earlier, and March was compensated with the earldom of Buchan, which was a poorer property and one which separated him territorially from the English friends with whom his family had been in treasonable association. When the Earl of Mar died in 1426 the crown took over that earldom, to the exclusion of the representatives of the lawful heir. The Earl of Douglas, too, though generally on good terms with James, was for a time under arrest.

That James's attitude to such nobles amounted to something more than mere acquisitiveness is suggested by other aspects of his policy. He endeavoured to strengthen the non-noble element in parliament, first of all by ordaining that all who held land of the King should attend and then by providing that the 'small barons and free tenants' should be relieved from personal attendance but that representatives should instead be sent from each sheriffdom. No such system of representation became effective for more than another century and a half, but it has often been suggested that James thought in terms of a parliament in which the burgesses and the representatives of the lesser landholders should together form a body comparable to the English House of Commons and provide a stronger complement to the prelates and peers than the burgesses alone could provide. It is also noticeable that a change was made in the system of administering the revenues. Previously the chamberlain, who had judicial as well as financial functions, had been the most powerful of the crown's ministers, and the office had been held for forty years or so by the elder Albany and then by his son John. But after John's death the office, shorn of most of its power, went to a man of much lower social standing, Sir John Forrester, while the chief functions in the control of finance were divided between two other officials, the treasurer and the comptroller.

This reorganisation of offices was connected with other changes in financial administration. Part of James's task was to recover and conserve the traditional sources of income, on which far too many inroads had been made during the Albany régime. Pensions or allowances had been made to individuals directly from the customs, the ferms or rents payable by some burghs had been diverted to private pockets. This was to stop. All moneys were first to come to the exchequer, where those with pretensions to allowances from them could submit their claims for scrutiny. As a result of this tightening-up, the actual income from the customs seems to have been about twice as much after James's return as it had been under Murdoch. Somewhat similarly, investigation was to be made of the titles of those who were in possession of lands which had once been the property of the crown. But there was also a great extension of the crown's holdings of land, because, as a result of the numerous forfeitures, the earldoms of Fife, Lennox, Strathearn, March and Mar all came into the hands of the King. If James was thus ruthless and acquisitive in relation to the greater men, he did not spare lesser men either, for, unlike Albany, he scorned the unpopularity which taxation would incur. The parliament of 1424 imposed a tax of 1*s.* in the pound on all land-rents and goods, to raise money to pay the King's ransom. The incomplete state of the records makes it impossible to determine how much was raised in this way, but we do know that, on the one hand, little of the ransom was ever paid, and, on the other, that the taxation was considered a grievous burden. A similar tax was imposed again in 1431. In 1436 a different expedient was tried—something like the 'benevolence' known in England: that is, the King's richer subjects and more prosperous towns were prevailed on to make a voluntary grant. We are told that they did so 'joyfully and gratefully'; but the King who had mulcted them was murdered in the following year.

Besides directly recovering and enlarging the royal property and levying taxes, there were ways of conserving the resources of the kingdom, to the indirect enrichment of the crown. Provision was made, for example, for the destruction of the nests of crows 'that dois gret skaithe [damage] apone cornis', for the organising of wolf-hunts and for a close-season for certain game; and there were penalties for the destruction of green wood, fruit-trees and dovecotes. Positively, every man was to have an ox in the plough or else to delve so much land; and every man who had a full plough team of eight oxen was to sow a specified quantity of wheat, pease or beans. It is not surprising, either, that James passed a number of acts designed to limit the export of bullion from the country and to encourage its import. One aspect of this was legislation which dealt with the excursions of the Scottish clergy, who were apt to go off to the great market of promotion at Rome, taking good Scottish money with them. James's first parliament ordained that no clerk was to pass beyond the sea without the royal consent, and that anyone taking gold or silver out of the realm was to pay a custom of 3*s.* 4*d.* in the pound. In 1427 it became the law that either clerks or laymen who required foreign currency had to make the necessary exchange within Scotland and give notice to the chancellor or the chamberlain.

James's obvious solicitude for law and order may have stemmed from a sense of justice which was genuine enough. He did appoint an advocate to act in the law courts on behalf of poor litigants, and one of his acts reflected a concern for the security of tenants in their holdings. According to one of the most frequently quoted passages from any Scottish chronicler, James declared on returning to his kingdom that 'if God give me life, though it be but the life of a dog, then throughout all Scotland, with His help, will I make the key keep the castle and the bracken bush the cow'. The hand of a man so resolved is to be seen in the first parliament of his reign, which met on 26 May 1424, less than seven weeks after his arrival—the earliest possible date, since parliament met on a summons of forty days. The first statute to be passed, after the customary assurance to the Church, was to the effect that 'ferme and sikkir [sure] pece be kepit and haldin throu all the realme'. But the King's solicitude for law and order was not unconnected with the forceful ruthlessness he showed against his nobles, for that same act was followed by legislation against those who levied private war, those who rebelled against the King, and those who were backward in supporting him against rebels. In later acts he was concerned not only to ensure the punishment of the actual committers of crimes, but to deal effectively with those who aided and abetted them, received and protected them.

Moreover, the law was to apply equally throughout the length and breadth of the land. In 1426, so it was formally declared, all the King's lieges were to be governed by the King's laws and the laws of the realm and not under any particular laws or special privileges or by the laws of other countries or realms. Possibly this enactment was aimed especially at Galloway, where some local laws had operated, and it is of some relevance that in the same reign an act was passed that the diocese of Galloway, although it had hitherto been ecclesiastically subject to the archbishopric of York, should now be treated in the same way as the rest of Scotland. But the act for uniformity of law would apply also to the West Highlands and Islands, where local customs prevailed and the King's laws did not always run, and which, indeed, had not yet been fully integrated into the Scottish realm. The distinction, in practice if not in law, between Lowlands and Highlands was expressly admitted in an act of 1425, stating that it was impracticable to apply to the Highlands certain regulations for compensation in the event of the infliction of injuries, for 'the hieland men commonly reft and slew ilk ane utheris [seized goods by force and slew each other]'.

James applied the strong hand to Highland chiefs as he applied it to Lowland nobles, for in 1428 he summoned a number of chiefs 'warily and singly' to the castle of Inverness and there arrested them. Three were executed, the others released after a brief imprisonment. The Lord of the Isles, the leading chief in the west, was attached for a time to the royal household, but he evidently found court life uncongenial and soon escaped to start a rebellion. He was captured and imprisoned, but other disorders arose and went on for years. Like all wise Scottish rulers, James I saw that he could never control the West Highlands unless he could cut communications between that area and Ireland, in which Scottish rebels could easily find refuge and from which they might draw assistance. The escape to Ireland of Duke Murdoch's son, James, after his rebellion, illustrated the danger. An act of 1426, ordaining that no ships were to cross to Ireland without the King's special leave, may have been an act which could not be enforced, but it is an indication of an intelligent approach. All in all there is nothing to show that James I made much lasting impression on the Highlands.

James was not content to pronounce in favour of a uniform legal system. He was also concerned to strengthen the machinery by which the legal system operated and the law was administered, and to do so in the interests of all classes of his subjects. One of his first acts was to the effect that there should be officers and ministers of law throughout the realm to do justice to the commons, and later acts provided that judges were to do justice to rich and poor without fraud or favour and that no one should come to any court with a band of followers who might overawe the judges. Apart from trying to strengthen the machinery of the local law courts, there was a reform of the central civil judicature, for an act of 1426 provided for a court under the chancellor, consisting of certain persons chosen by the King from the three estates and holding three sessions in the year where the King commanded them. This was to be a permanent or semi-permanent court, supplementary to the 'auditors of causes' who were appointed by parliament and operated only while parliament was sitting, but the judges were not to be salaried—they were only to receive their expenses from the parties whose suits were defeated. Evidence is scanty, but it seems that this 'session' did work at least as long as James lived.

Even when an account has been given of the repression of nobles, financial exactions, the legislation of no less than thirteen parliaments or general councils, and judicial and parliamentary reforms, that is not the whole tale of the activities during his thirteen years of rule of this vigorous and sturdy man. The foundations of an interest in letters had been laid before James left Scotland as a boy, for he had received some of his education under the care of Henry Wardlaw, the Bishop who a few years later was to found Scotland's first university at St Andrews. His years in England added to his attainments in scholarship and culture. It is by no means clear that he wrote any other substantial poem besides the *Kingis Quair*, though others have been attributed to him, but he was something of a musician as well as a poet, and a Scottish chronicler said that he was 'like another Orpheus'. It was only to be expected that when he settled in Scotland he would take an interest in the university which Bishop Wardlaw had founded. At one stage he considered removing it from St Andrews, a site hallowed by ancient ecclesiastical associations but not very convenient of access, to a more central position at Perth, a town which he evidently regarded as something like a capital. Finally, however, he confirmed the privileges of the university at its existing site, and he is said, by a later writer, to have been sufficiently interested to attend some of the professors' lectures.

James had peculiar opportunities to shape a decisive policy in ecclesiastical affairs. The position was influenced by two features—first, the dissemination of a good deal of heresy, after a generation which had seen Wycliff in England and Hus in Bohemia, and, second, the aftermath of the Great Schism (1378–1417), during which two, and sometimes three, rival popes had competed for the allegiance of the kingdoms of Western Europe. The first known execution of a heretic in Scotland had taken place under the governorship of the elder Albany, of whom it was said that

He was a constant catholike,
All Lollard he hated and heretik.

James's attachment to orthodoxy was not in any doubt either, and in the Lancastrian England where he had learned so much a statute had been passed *De heretico comburendo*. The second known execution of a heretic in Scotland took place during his personal reign. But James combined doctrinal conservatism with a somewhat independent line in relation to the pope. There had been a general expectation that the end of the Schism would be followed by constitutional government in the Church, to the extent that the popes would be subject to General Councils, and in Scotland, which had been one of the last countries to abandon support of an anti-pope, conciliar opinions were particularly strong. The pope appointed at the close of the Schism was, however, a masterful pontiff, who soon made it clear that he was going to revive the centralising policy which his predecessors had followed and that he was not going to be overruled by councils. A clash was inevitable with the King of Scots, as masterful a man in his way as the pope was. James legislated against the Scottish churchmen's habit of going to Rome to seek appointments, partly with a view to keeping money in the country but partly to protect the rights of native patrons of benefices, including himself. The friction with the papacy which naturally resulted led James to support the Council of Basel, which tried to curb the autocracy of the pope and ultimately set up a fresh anti-pope. James's aims were not entirely self-seeking, for he also showed that he had the good of the Church at heart. He imitated Henry V, whose prisoner he had lately been, by writing in scathing terms to the heads of Scottish religious houses to tell them that if they did not reform themselves they might find their endowments in jeopardy. As an object lesson to them he founded in his favourite town of Perth Scotland's only community of the strict Carthusian order—the order which boasted that it never required to be reformed because it was never deformed.

James's interests could best be served by the maintenance of peace with other countries, and he did not go to war until nearly the end of his reign. Some light is thrown on Scottish foreign policy by the marriages arranged for his daughters (some of them, admittedly, after his own death). The eldest, Margaret, was married when she was twelve—as it turned out, very unhappily—to the Dauphin of France, afterwards Louis XI, and she died before he became King. Isabella married Francis, Duke of Britanny, and Eleanor married Sigismund, Duke of Austria. Two other daughters married minor continental notables. Joan, who was dumb, and became the wife of the first Earl of Morton, was the only one not married abroad, though one of her sisters took the Earl of Huntly for her second husband. The pattern suggests that Scottish Kings were regarded by contemporaries as princes of some consequence, and the French marriage of Margaret may indicate that, although James I himself had married an English princess, he was not disposed to depart from Scotland's traditional foreign policy by seeking a lasting alliance with England at the expense of the established link with France. In 1436 he made his solitary experiment in foreign warfare, by laying siege to Roxburgh, which had been in English hands for a century. The expedition was a complete fiasco, possibly because reports of disaffection in the heart of his kingdom compelled James to return from the frontier. At the very least, the episode suggests that the King's control over nobles and people was far from complete, and his ignominious retreat must have reacted adversely on his prestige.

James's murder followed at the beginning of the next year. The ringleader in the conspiracy was Sir Robert Graham, who had personally felt the weight of the King's displeasure at the beginning of the reign; since then he had publicly denounced James as a tyrant and had taken refuge in the Highlands, where it was not difficult to muster a force ready for any act of violence. The King to some extent played into Graham's hands by deciding to spend the Christmas of 1436 in the Dominican friary at Perth, which was so ready of access from the Highlands. It is picturesquely related that James was warned of danger by a Celtic seeress (who may, in fact, have acquired her information from one of Graham's Highlanders and not by any occult means), but he persisted in his plans. There were traitors in the royal household, who bridged the moat with planks and removed the bars from the doors, so that when the conspirators burst in, about midnight on 20 February, they met with no obstacle except—according to later legend—a frail arm which one of the Queen's ladies thrust through the staples on the door of the royal apartment. In the brief respite, James tore up part of the flooring and leaped down into an underground vault or drain. Unluckily for

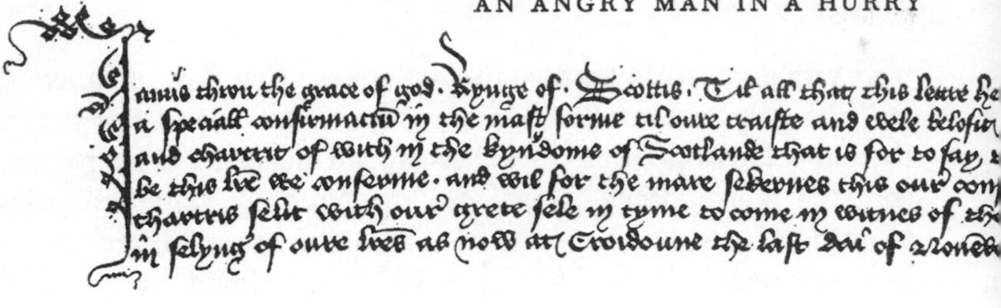

4 James I's 'proper hand'

him, he had recently caused the egress from this chamber to be walled up because his tennis balls had sometimes been lost there. Even so, the murderers were withdrawing to seek their victim elsewhere when James made premature attempts to emerge from his refuge, and the murderers returned to find him struggling to climb back into the room. The King had been described some years earlier as 'oppressed by his excessive corpulence', but, although he was unarmed, he left his mark on his assailants before they were able to despatch him, with, so it is said, sixteen wounds. His body was buried in his recently founded Charterhouse at Perth, his heart was taken on a pilgrimage to the Holy Land and brought back by a knight of Rhodes.

It is not hard to see that James had antagonised many powerful interests in his kingdom. The inroads which the nobles had become accustomed to make on crown lands and revenues had been checked, their rights of jurisdiction may have been infringed by some of the legal reforms, the experiences of the Albanys, of Strathearn and of March must have suggested that none of them could feel completely secure in his dignities and property. Human nature being what it is, there must have been some who regretted the good old days of the Albanys, when the government was too easy-going to check them. Moreover, there was the novelty of the taxations, which affected more than the nobles, and it may have been especially unpopular that taxation raised to pay off the King's ransom was diverted to other ends. Then this diversion, involving the non-payment of the ransom, meant that hostages were retained in England, a fact which can hardly have increased the King's popularity with their kinsmen.

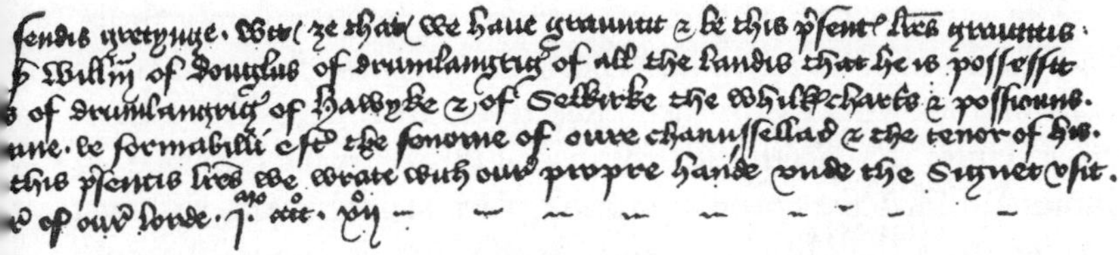
sendis gretynge. Wit ȝe that we haue grauntit & be this p̄sent l̄res grauntis
to Willm̄ of Douglas of Drumlanrig of all the landis that he is possessit
of Drumlanrig of Hawyke & of Selkirke the whilk chartris & possiouns
... the tenoure of oure chanusellad & the tenor of his
this p̄sentis lres we wrate with oure propre hande vnder the Signet
of oure lorde ...

Besides, James's methods were not always in keeping with his aims, or at any rate his better aims. Andrew Lang characterised James as 'the ablest and not the most scrupulous of the Stewarts' and added that 'the dramatic story of his death has won him a sympathy which his aims deserve better than his methods'.* His proceedings seem to have been coloured by personal vindictiveness and an angry temper, and his financial policy is alleged to have arisen in part from personal cupidity and not only from a statesmanlike wish to restore the crown's strength and the country's stability. It appears, too, that he borrowed money which he failed to repay, and one of his assassins was a burgess of Perth to whom he owed money.

It has, however, always been believed that the assassins were moved by family feud and dynastic ambitions. Sir Robert Graham, the ringleader, was the uncle of Malise Graham, the senior representative of the Euphemia Ross line, who had been disappointed of the earldom of Strathearn and had been left as a hostage in England. But Malise was not the statutory heir to the throne, as his royal descent was through his mother, and Sir Robert Graham therefore intrigued also with the Earl of Atholl, who, as the nearest male descendant of Euphemia Ross, was heir after the son of James I. Atholl seems on the whole to have been on good terms with James, despite the fact that his son was a hostage in England, but his attitude may have changed after his son's death about 1434. Increasing influence may then have been exerted over him by his grandson, Sir Robert Stewart, in whom Graham saw a future King should James be eliminated and James's son disposed of or ignored.

*Andrew Lang, *History of Scotland*, i, 300

The assassination of James I proved to be completely futile, and there seems never to have been the slightest chance that the conspirators would gain their objectives. In little over a month after James I's death, his six-year-old son was crowned as James II. That the coronation took place at Holyrood, so much farther from the Highlands than Scone was, is almost the only indication that there was any apprehension about the security of the dynasty. The murderers of the King had been seized without difficulty, and they were put to death with cruelties unparalleled in Scottish history. The only crown which Atholl gained was a crown of red-hot iron placed on his head as part of his torture,* his grandson perished with him, and the male line of Euphemia Ross was extinguished. This outcome was no doubt the consequence of the resolution of Queen Joan to assert the rights of her child, but she could not have achieved much single-handed, and the conclusion is inescapable that a substantial body of influential opinion favoured the title of the descendants of Elizabeth Mure, even if it did not approve of the policies of the late King.

In many ways, James I may have charted the course for his successors for two centuries, though if we knew more about earlier statutes it might emerge that much of his well-intentioned legislation had been anticipated by David II and even by Robert I. At any rate, in succeeding years the aims remained much the same. One thing the conspiracy of 1437 did was to demonstrate that a royal policy of reckless acquisitiveness towards the nobles was apt to provoke a sharp reaction. The fate of James I was a lesson which was lost on James V and Charles I, each of whom, at intervals of about a century, pursued courses not unlike those of James I and met disaster in consequence. But wiser monarchs adopted other methods to achieve their aims. In the end, the sixth James very largely succeeded in carrying out the policy which the first James had designed.

*Other accounts say that a paper crown was placed on his head when he was tortured and that an iron crown surmounted his skull when it was publicly displayed in Edinburgh

5

The Stewart and the Douglas: James II, 1437-60

For the reign of James I the evidence at the historian's disposal can hardly be called ample, and there are many points where it leaves us at a loss, unable to determine the precise course of events and the reason why things happened as they did; nor can we always understand exactly what was at issue between the King and his opponents. But, in spite of this, a fairly clear general picture, a pattern with some kind of meaning, does emerge. After the death of James I, however, we enter on a period when reliable narrative sources are scanty and records are still inadequate. Consequently, the very course of events is at times impossible to follow; it is hard indeed to detect any pattern at all; and above all, the motives which shaped the actions and policies of both the government and its opponents are so uncertain as to be unintelligible. It is all rather like watching a play in an unknown language, and watching it, too, by a rather fitful light: that is, we see only parts of the action, and the thoughts lying behind that action are concealed from us.

James had been born at Holyrood on 16 October 1430 and was therefore only six years old when he succeeded his father. Of his education nothing is known, and his character can only be inferred from his actions. Nor do we have any description of his appearance, though there is a contemporary sketch of him, apparently as a youth; and the only physical feature in his person about which we have information is a large birthmark which caused him to be known as 'James of the Fiery Face'. In 1449 James married Mary, only daughter of Arnold, Duke of Gueldres, and by her had six children. Of their four sons, one, David, died young, and the others—James III, the Duke of Albany and the Earl of Mar—figure in history. One daughter, Mary, was married first to Thomas, Lord Boyd, and secondly to James, Lord Hamilton; the other, Margaret, was married, or at least betrothed, to Lord Crichton. Mary of Gueldres, coming from a land of wealth where the arts flourished, almost certainly made a mark on the culture of her adopted country, and both her piety and her patronage of artists and craftsmen were transmitted to her son, James III. It can also be suggested—though it is only a matter of inference—that she was possessed of considerable political intelligence which she put at the service of her husband.

It was very shortly before his marriage that James II, at the age of eighteen, first became personally an active agent in policy and government, and the situation which confronted him then had a certain resemblance to that which his father had had to deal with when he returned from England in 1424. Once again power and office had been engrossed by a single family. But the Livingstons, who had risen to eminence in James II's minority, were not, like the Albanys, of the royal house, and, far from being competitors for the crown, were not even of the highest rank among the nobility. The events through which such a family had established its ascendancy are obscure. At first after James I's death, his widow, Queen Joan, was associated in the administration with the fifth Earl of Douglas and Bishop Cameron of Glasgow, who was chancellor; but in May 1439 Cameron was replaced as chancellor by Sir William Crichton and in the following month Douglas died. Shortly afterwards the Queen married Sir James Stewart of Lorne. This marriage to a subject, and one not of the first rank, may have been thought to disqualify the Queen from any further part in government, and if she and her husband had any thought of seizing power they were thwarted by Sir Alexander Livingston, who arrested them and let them go only on condition that they were not to retain custody of the young King. Livingston and Chancellor Crichton for a time competed for the keeping of the King's person, then for a time collaborated, but by 1445 Livingston had become the senior partner in the alliance and Crichton was ousted from the chancellorship. By 1449 the Livingstons were well entrenched in office. Sir Alexander was justiciar; Sir James was chamberlain; Robert Livingston of Linlithgow was comptroller; John Livingston was master of the mint; and the captains of the castles of Stirling, Dumbarton, Doune and Methven were all Livingstons. They obviously had a tight grip on government finance, they controlled much crown property, and in Stirling and Dumbarton they held two of the castles which could be reckoned among the keys of the kingdom.

Their fall was sudden and spectacular. On Monday, 23 September 1449, we are told by a contemporary chronicler, 'James of Levingstoun was arrestit be the King, and Robyn [Livingston of] Kalendar, capitane of Dunbertane, and Johne of Levingstoun, capitane of the castell of Doune, and David Levingstoun of the Greneyardis, with syndry uthiris. And sone after this, Schir Alexander Levingstoun was arrestit, and Robyn of Levingstoun of Lithgow, that tyme comptrollar. And James and his brother Alexander and Robyn of Lithgow war put in the Blacknes, and thair gudis tane within xl dayis in all places, and put under arrest, and all thair gudis that pertenit to that party. And all officeris that war put in be thaim war clerlie put out of all officis, and all put doun that thai put up. And this was a gret ferlie [marvel].'* It was a change of government with a vengeance.

The circumstances of the Livingstons' fall are as obscure as those of their rise to power. We do not know the grounds, either real or ostensible, on which they were thus arrested and two of them put to death. But, as had been the case with some of James I's

**Auchinleck Chronicle*, quoted A. I. Dunlop, *Bishop Kennedy* (1950), 106

actions, the reason for the proceedings against the Livingstons may have been the inroads they had been making on the resources of the crown. One of the Livingstons to be executed was captain of Methven Castle, the other was custumar of Linlithgow: now, the castle of Methven and the customs of Linlithgow were part of the marriage portion of Mary of Gueldres, who had arrived in Scotland in June 1449 and was married to James on 3 July, and, on the day after the Livingstons' execution, parliament confirmed the marriage portion. It would seem that it had been forcibly brought home to James that financially as otherwise he was too much at the mercy of the Livingstons, and it may even be possible to detect the hand of the new Queen, stimulating her husband to satisfy her financial claims and at the same time assert his authority. Even so, the overthrow of the Livingstons was thought so high-handed that some justification was felt necessary, and a supplication to the pope stated that Livingston of Callendar had been guilty of 'rebellion and other excesses'. Any tendency to theorise about high principles on the part of the King and his advisers may, besides, be checked when it is noted that James owed the Comptroller the sum of £1,000 and that by the death and forfeiture of his creditor he was absolved from any need to repay the sum.

Possibly the greatest mystery is how a King of Scots, at the age of eighteen, had the means to deal with a powerful family in such a sudden and ruthless manner. But this is tied up with the question how the Livingstons had themselves established their ascendancy and had ousted Crichton and other competitors for office. It may be that the key is to be found in the manœuvrings of the great house of Douglas. There are certainly reasons for believing that the eighth Earl of Douglas had helped to set Sir Alexander Livingston up and that he may have decided in 1449 to pull him down; indeed, the Douglases may all along have been the real power behind the Livingstons.

It was certainly the Douglases, and not the Livingstons or any other lesser family, who constituted the significant threat to the crown in this reign. Their power, influence and prestige had been growing ever since the period of the War of Independence. Sir William Douglas, who took the national side against England and died in the Tower of London, had married the daughter of James the High Steward, and his son by that marriage was 'the good Sir James', who was one of Robert Bruce's most energetic lieutenants. Douglas's work in liberating Scotland was largely in the southern parts of the country, and it was there that he received his great territorial rewards—Jedburgh, Ettrick Forest, Lauderdale, Eskdale and Teviotdale. Although the family did not attain the dignity of an earldom until 1357, those lands were granted on highly privileged terms which already made Douglas more than an ordinary subject. The first Earl of Douglas, a nephew of Sir James, established a French connection which the family long retained, for he fought at Poitiers and was knighted by King John of France. His son James, the second Earl, was a ringleader in the attacks which were made on England, with French help, in Robert II's reign, and he died in battle against Percy ('Hotspur') at Otterburn, in 1388. The third Earl, Archibald the Grim, a natural son of the good Sir James, had acquired the modern county of Kirkcudbright from the King in 1369, and in 1372 he had purchased the earldom of Wigtown from Thomas Fleming, so that the lands of the old lordship of Galloway were brought together under Douglas rule. The fourth Earl continued and strengthened the French connection of the house and was the most distinguished of the whole line, for, after leading Scottish forces to France during the captivity of James I, he became lieutenant-general of the French army and died in 1424 with the title of Duke of Touraine. The renown of the Douglases as warriors is commemorated not only in folk tales about 'the good Sir James' and in the Ballad of Chevy Chase which relates how 'a dead man won a fight' at Otterburn, but also in Shakespeare, who referred to

brave Archibald,
That ever valiant and approved Scot

and to

renowned Douglas, whose high deeds,

Whose hot incursions and great name in arms
Holds from all soldiers chief majority
And military title capital
*Through all the kingdoms that acknowledge Christ.**

The importance of the Douglases arose not only from their territorial possessions and their international reputation as warriors, but also from their place in the royal succession. They had all along been intermarrying with the Stewarts. The mother of 'the good Sir James' was a daughter of the Steward; the second Earl married a daughter of Robert II by his first wife, the fourth Earl married the eldest daughter of Robert III, and a daughter of the third Earl married David, Duke of Rothesay, elder son of Robert III. But it was perhaps more important that the fifth Earl of Douglas married Euphemia, granddaughter of David, Earl of Strathearn, the elder son of Robert II by his second marriage to Euphemia Ross; this Countess of Douglas was the sister of Malise, Earl of Strathearn and Menteith, who was the senior representative of the Euphemia Ross line. The events of 1437 immensely strengthened the Douglas position in relation to the succession. The death of James I and the extinction of the Atholl line by the execution of Earl Walter and his grandson meant that the six-year-old James II was the only surviving descendant of Robert II in the male line and the only heir of entail under the Succession Act of 1373. Men must have asked where the heir of James II was to be found. The preference would almost certainly be for a male, although inheriting through a female, rather than for a female. The nearest male was possibly the fifth Earl of Douglas, representing the Elizabeth Mure line in his own person and the Euphemia Ross line in right of his wife, while Malise of Menteith was not merely an heir, but a possible rival, to James II. Malise had become a hostage for the unpaid ransom of James II and was still in England; besides, although he was to live until about 1490, throughout his long life he never seems to have pressed his claim to the succession and took little part in affairs, and it

**Henry IV*, *Part I*, Act I, scene i, and Act III, scene ii may perhaps be inferred that he was infirm either mentally or physically. The fifth Earl of Douglas had, indeed, engaged in some kind of negotiations with the Earl of Salisbury, the custodian of Malise; but, especially if Malise and his sons were disregarded, the Douglas line itself had a high place in the royal succession. It may be that when the fifth Earl of Douglas was appointed lieutenant of Scotland on the accession of James II he was being recognised not only as the first subject of the kingdom but also as heir presumptive.

When the fifth Earl died, in 1439, he was succeeded by his young son, William. It was this boy, and his brother, who were the victims of the 'Black Dinner' in Edinburgh Castle in 1440, when they were seized in the presence of the young King James II and hurried to execution. Their great-uncle, who succeeded as Earl James 'the Gross', was a party to their removal, but the murder may have had other purposes apart from the advancement of a wicked uncle. It represented an attempt to break the Douglas succession by eliminating the Earl (who, although only about sixteen, was already married) and his brother, and also to divide the Douglas inheritance, for, while the wicked uncle succeeded to the title of Earl and some of the estates, Galloway went to the sister of the murdered boys, Margaret, the Maid of Galloway. The two boys were descended from both of Robert II's marriages, and might be deemed heirs to whoever was rightful King—whether James II or Malise of Menteith.

But the 'Black Dinner', if it had any statesmanlike purpose, proved as futile as the murder of James I had been. When Earl James 'the Gross' died, his son, who succeeded as eighth Earl, married his cousin the Maid of Galloway, reunited the Douglas inheritance and recovered, in right of his wife, the family's place in the royal succession. Not only so, but the Douglas power extended in other directions. The second son of Earl James became Bishop of Aberdeen; his third son married the co-heiress to the earldom of Moray and succeeded to that earldom; Hugh, another son, became Earl of Ormond; the youngest son, John, succeeded to his father's lordship of Balveny, in Banffshire. The family was thus immensely strong territorially, from Galloway and the Borders right up to Moray and Ross.

Almost immediately on the overthrow of the Livingstons, the Earl of Douglas went abroad for some months, partly in order to visit Rome in the jubilee year of 1450. On his outward journey he was feasted by the Duke of Burgundy, on his way home he was entertained at the English court. What he may have sought in making contacts abroad does not appear, but his absence was certainly detrimental to his interests in Scotland. It happened that the old Countess of Douglas, widow of the fifth Earl, who had had a life-rent of Galloway, died at this time, and the crown took the opportunity to advance the families of Kennedy and Agnew in Galloway as a counterpoise to the Douglases. There are indications, too, of crown favour towards the Earl of Angus, who was warden of the east marches (while the Earl of Douglas was warden of the middle and west marches). Further, disturbances within Douglas's domains gave the crown an opportunity to intervene in the interests of order.

On Douglas's return from his travels abroad, there was no immediate breach with the King, but the reconciliation, if it was not merely on the surface, was short-lived. There were probably fresh intrigues with England, for the Earl's brother, James, paid a visit to that country in 1451, and in Scotland the Earl resumed an alliance with the Earl of Crawford and entered into a new bond with him and with the Earl of Ross, who was also Lord of the Isles. This bond threatened to produce a coalition more dangerous than any which had threatened the crown before. It led directly to an invitation to Douglas to sup with the King at Stirling. The Earl came under a safe conduct, but on his refusal to break the bond he was murdered by the King's own hand (22 February 1452). In one of its aspects, but only one, this was another item in the feud with the descendants of Euphemia Ross.

Even if the King knew that a Crawford-Ross-Douglas rebellion was going to break out, he did not, by the murder, prevent it. Indeed, what he can have hoped to gain it is impossible to say, and on the whole the likelihood is that the action was quite unpremeditated and wholly impolitic. If there had been a chance of a peaceful solution of the Douglas problem, there was no such chance now, and the problem itself became the more serious in that the new Earl, James, considered himself absolved from his allegiance to the crown. With his brother Ormond he rode into Stirling and there formally proclaimed the withdrawal of his allegiance to James Stewart, and he sent a message to King Henry VI of England offering to do homage to him instead. Not only was Douglas himself thus active, but his allies in the famous bond were stirring. A crisis was clearly approaching. Douglas obtained a dispensation allowing him to marry his brother's widow, the Maid of Galloway, so that the entire Douglas inheritance would be united again and the Earl of Douglas would once more be a representative of the Euphemia Ross line. Not only so, but while Douglas was in England in 1453 as a commissioner in negotiations regarding a truce, he brought about the liberation of Malise Graham, Earl of Menteith, the Maid of Galloway's uncle and senior representative of that rival royal line. This was the Douglas answer to the birth of a son to James's Queen in May 1452: the senior line, now likely to be perpetuated, was going to be directly challenged.

The fact that military operations started in 1455 may be accounted for by the effect on Scotland of what was happening in England. James II was a supporter of the Lancastrian dynasty, while Douglas was being cultivated by the Yorkists and had recently sent his ally, Lord Hamilton, to negotiate with the Duke of York. Now, the Yorkists decided to appeal to the sword at this point, and the battle of St Albans (22 May 1455) marks the beginning of the Wars of the Roses. The prospect of a dynastic war in England may have led Douglas to muster his adherents and challenge the Scottish King in that same spring. In England, the battle of St Albans ushered in a thirty years' conflict; but Scotland was more fortunate, and the contest between Stewart and Douglas was soon over.

The King dealt swift blows at the lands of Lord Hamilton, Douglas's ally, and then at the Douglas lands in Ettrick Forest, and the Douglases and their supporters were summoned to stand trial for treason. The Douglas castle of Abercorn, in West Lothian, besieged by the King, held out for a month against the bombardment of a 'a gret gun, the quhilk a Frenchemen schot richt wele', but was at last taken by storm. Douglas fled to England, leaving his brothers to carry on the war in the south-west of Scotland. They were defeated by the Earl of Angus at Arkinholm (1 May 1455); Moray was killed on the field and Ormond was captured and executed, while Balveny fled to England to join his brother. Other Douglas castles fell, and siege was laid to the island stronghold of Threave, in Kirkcudbrightshire, which held out against a 'great bombard' for some weeks but ultimately surrendered. Douglas meantime became a pensioner of the English King 'until he is restored to his heritage, taken from him by him who calls himself King of Scots'. The phrase shows that Douglas was not merely transferring his allegiance, but was disputing the claim of James Stewart to be King of Scots.

That the King had shown considerable initiative at one stage after another in the critical struggle against the house of Douglas is evident. There are indications, too, in the complex and often obscure manœuvrings, of a political intelligence which made the fullest use of all the opportunities open to the crown. According to one sixteenth-century writer, when James was faced with the reinforcement of the Douglas position through the marriage of the ninth Earl to the Maid of Galloway and the liberation of Malise Graham, he contemplated giving up the struggle and withdrawing from the country, but another chronicler says that the King deliberately spread a report that he was intending to flee the country in order to lull his enemies into a false sense of security. According to an unlikely tale by an over-picturesque narrator, James went in his despair to Bishop Kennedy of St Andrews, who showed him, by taking up a sheaf of arrows, that although his enemies were irresistible when united, they could be broken one by one. The story is at least symbolic, for this was precisely the policy which James followed, and which he had initiated at least as early as 1452. He was able to play on the jealousies and rivalries between one noble house and another, and apparently encouraged the Gordons against the Lindsays, so that the Earl of Huntly took the field on the King's behalf in 1452 against Douglas's ally Crawford and routed him. James even split the Douglas interest itself, to the extent that he raised up the Earl of Angus, the 'Red Douglas' (a descendant of an illegitimate son of the first Earl of Douglas), against the 'Black Douglases'. At a parliament in June 1452, when Crawford was forfeited, there was a distribution of titles and lands which looks like the exploitation of the crown's patronage in a large-scale bid for support, by rewarding services rendered or procuring promises of future assistance. There was another striking example of the King's pursuance of Kennedy's advice in 1455, when James was able to play on the irresolution of Lord Hamilton, who had evidently an important part assigned to him in Douglas's plans. Hamilton declined to follow Douglas to the extent of transferring his allegiance to England, and when military operations started he evidently lost his nerve and threw himself on King James's mercy, leaving 'the Earl of Douglas all begylit'.

The same general principle of dividing the nobility and raising up certain families to a new eminence may possibly lie behind some significant developments in the Scottish peerage which belong to this reign. With the failure of James I's attempt to secure either the general attendance of tenants-in-chief in parliament or a system of representation of the lesser barons and freeholders, there had come to be a sharper distinction than before between those who were summoned personally to parliament and those who were not, and the former attained a new dignity as 'Lords of Parliament', forming a peerage of a lower grade than the earls. About fourteen such lords had made their appearance before James II took over the direction of affairs, and during his active reign another eight lairds were raised to this new dignity, evidently as part of the process of organising a royal party. It is equally, or even more, notable that James thought it desirable to raise proportionately in rank some of those who held older lordships, and this involved the appearance in some numbers of what may be called honorific earldoms. There had been two cases during the King's minority, those of Huntly and Ormond (1444–45). In 1452, Hay of Errol, the Constable, was created Earl of Errol, and in the later years of the reign there appeared new earldoms of Argyll, Marischal, Morton and Rothes, while the old earldoms of Atholl and Caithness were revived. Not content with those marks of royal patronage, James married one of his sisters to the Earl of Huntly and another to James Douglas of Dalkeith, who became Earl of Morton. By this time a large proportion of the older earldoms, in which a family with a long native pedigree was associated with an ancient territorial division of the country and its inhabitants, had become dormant or were vested in the crown: Buchan, Carrick, Dunbar, Fife, Lennox, Mar, Moray and Strathearn. Most of those which survived as separate entities had passed to new families with, at most, a tenuous connection with the ancient lines: Angus, Atholl, Caithness, Menteith and Ross. The only earldom in which the ancient dynasty continued in the male line was Sutherland. The pattern had changed radically from the days of Alexander III, and even from the previous century. Those very few great magnates whose title represented extensive power over a large block of territory—Argyll and Huntly are the most conspicuous examples—owed nothing to the tradition of the ancient earls of Celtic times.

The King's resolution in framing policy and acting upon it, and the King's diplomacy in his dealings with his mighty subjects, clearly played their parts in James II's success. But the problem was, in part at least, a military one, and the solution was to be found in the use of artillery. Before the introduction of artillery, the advantage lay with the defence, and the noble in his stone castle was able to defy the King; but, with the introduction and improvement of artillery, the advantage equally clearly passed to the attack, and the crown's opportunity had come. The first mention of artillery in Scottish record was in 1384, when 'an instrument called a gun' was bought for the castle of Edinburgh at a cost of only £4. Our scanty evidence next reveals that in 1430 James I imported 'a huge bombard of brass' from

Flanders. But it is in James II's reign that artillery became peculiarly important, and indeed decisive. It has been suggested that the King's marriage to Mary of Gueldres not only brought him face to face with a full realisation of the power of the Livingstons, but also put into his hands the means of bringing about their sudden downfall, for as part of his wife's marriage portion he acquired guns made by the expert smiths and founders of the Low Countries, a weapon to which his subjects could not reply. It was probably at some time in this reign, too, that Scotland acquired that massive piece of ordnance called Mons Meg which is still to be seen in Edinburgh Castle and for which generations of Scots had an almost superstitious veneration. Various improbable tales have circulated about its having been the production of a local smith when James was engaged on the siege of Threave, but, apart from the evidence of the name Mons Meg itself, a comparison of her design and dimensions with those of her slightly larger sister, Dulle Griet at Ghent, is conclusive about her origins.

This military problem also involved a financial problem. Feudal charters, granted before artillery had been thought of, had provided for the service of knights or of archers, but guns were not a feudal prestation, and the most the King could do was to request his feudatories to supply cannon, as he did in 1456. Failing any such 'benevolence', cannon could be obtained only if money could be found to pay for them. Equally, although soldiers of a kind could be procured either through the machinery of feudal tenure or by means of the general musters which were supposed to be attended by all men between sixteen and sixty, a more efficient force for a prolonged campaign could be obtained only by the employment of paid men—'wagers'—and this again meant money. The experience of James I had shown that it was inexpedient to levy taxation, for the yield in revenue would not compensate for the resulting unpopularity.

If the crown was to have the necessary money, it had to have land, which was still the main source of wealth. In order to meet the increasing expenses of government, more especially when war expenditure and particularly artillery were concerned, there was more need than ever to husband and augment the royal resources. Now, James II had acquired broad lands on the fall of the Black Douglases, so adding substantially to the territory acquired by his father; but the question was, were such properties to be retained by the crown? On the overthrow of the Douglases, the parliament of August 1455 passed an important act relating to the endowment of the crown. The preamble acknowledged that the well-being of the state was bound up with the strength of the crown, and the act ordained in the first place that for the convenience of the King's residence and maintenance on his travels through the realm certain lordships and castles should be perpetually annexed to the crown. Apart from the King's convenience on his movements throughout his realm, it was desirable that there should be points of royal property in each part of the country. The act went on to declare that all customs vested in the crown at the death of James I should remain irrevocably with his successors, and it gave a list of the lordships and castles which were likewise annexed—Ettrick, Galloway and lands in the north, forfeited by the Douglases; the three key fortresses of Edinburgh, Stirling and Dumbarton, and two strategic castles in the north, Inverness and Urquhart; the earldoms of Fife and Strathearn and the lordship of Brechin. A determined effort was thus made to exalt the monarchy above the level of the great feudatories. It was necessary to ensure that succeeding princes should not throw away the inheritance so hardly gained, and it was therefore enacted that any alienations of the annexed lordships and castles should be invalid and that kings on their accession should swear to observe the statute, that is, to keep their patrimony unimpaired. Finally, all grants of heritable offices made since the death of James I were revoked; hereditary wardenships of the marches were forbidden; all regalities then vested in the crown were merged in the sheriffdoms, while no new regalities were to be created except with the consent of parliament. This was all a declaration of policy rather than an effective enactment, but it showed that James II, or his advisers, had a clear grasp of the sources of the weakness of the crown and of the means by which it might be strengthened.

After this point, James showed signs of pursuing a policy of the further aggrandisement of the crown and perhaps of vainglorious ambition. Between 1455 and 1457 he paid many visits to the west and north, no doubt to strengthen royal authority there, but partly to ensure acquiescence in an aggressive foreign policy. He attacked the Isle of Man and took a lofty line in negotiating with Norway over the tribute owing to that kingdom for the Western Isles. It was therefore politic to treat the Lord of the Isles (and Earl of Ross) with some generosity. Within Scotland itself, James's acquisitions seem to have whetted his appetite, and, while he used some earldoms to ennoble and enrich his faithful supporters, he pursued a policy of adding more to the crown's holdings. In the earldom of Mar, the claimant was Sir Robert Erskine, heir of the last Countess of Mar, but he had been set aside by James I in 1435. Now, in 1457, an assize, meeting in the tolbooth of Aberdeen in presence of the King, rejected the claims of Erskine and found that the lands of Mar were of right vested in the crown. No doubt there was intimidation, or possibly bribery, but the outcome was that the descendants of Sir Robert Erskine were excluded from the earldom until 1565 and at this stage it was settled on one of the King's sons. Somewhat similarly, claimants to the earldom of Moray were ignored, and it was settled on another of the King's sons.

In the ten years or so of his personal reign, before his death in his thirtieth year, James II had achieved a remarkable success. Events, in all their obscurity, show many indications of an intelligently directed policy. In some respects his task had been harder than his father's. James I's policy had all along been aggressive, and the shock of his tactics seems to have left the barons somewhat breathless and incapable of rallying in force against him. James II, by contrast, was equally clearly for some years under a serious threat from nobles who had recovered their nerve and took concerted action to defy him. But, with all James's skill, it is hard to deny that the crown might have come much worse out of the struggle had its chief enemies, the Douglases, been more resolute. There was probably no agreement on any plan to supersede James Stewart; and even if it had been agreed that he should be superseded, who was to succeed him—Malise of Menteith, as the senior, but ineffectual, representative of the second marriage of Robert II, or the Douglas husband of the Maid of Galloway as representing both lines of descent from Robert II? It may be that the crown was saved by the lack of clearly understood objectives on the part of the Douglases almost as much as by any merits on the part of the King and his government.

It is an interesting commentary on James's success, and on the situation after 1455, that in 1458, in a somewhat remarkable statement, parliament gave the King a testimonial. All rebels and breakers of the King's justice, it was stated, had been removed, 'no masterful party remaining', and the King was exhorted to be inclined to the execution of the statutes recently passed, 'that God may be empleased of him, and all his lieges may pray for him to God and give thanks to Him that sends them such a prince to be their governor and defender'. It is true that, apart from the murder of Douglas, James had been more scrupulous than his father, he had at no stage conducted anything like a reign of terror, and he may have been trusted as his father had never been. Certainly he had a good deal of support from some of the nobles. But, no doubt because of the excellent legislation of his reign, his government may have commanded a widespread attachment from all classes. There is, at any rate, ample evidence of good intentions, and some of substantial achievement. There is some reason to believe that, had James lived longer, he might have moved towards the kind of ruthless acquisitiveness which had been fatal to his father and was to be fatal again to James V. But he was cut off while his statesmanship was still foremost in men's minds.

The incident which led to his death was in some sense an extension of the link between the English contest of York and Lancaster and the Scottish contest of Stewart and Douglas. On 10 July 1460 the Lancastrian Henry VI was defeated and captured at Northampton, and James, who had favoured his cause, seized the opportunity to embarrass the new English government and recover some of *Scotia irredenta* by besieging Roxburgh Castle. On 3 August, as he watched the discharge of one of his beloved bombards, one of the wedges used to tighten the iron hoops around the barrel flew off and killed James of the Fiery Face.

5 Stirling Castle
From John Slezer, 'Theatrum Scotiae'

6

The Royal Enigma: James III, 1460-88

'Death of James II; tumult in Edinburgh', reads the laconic entry in a chronicle. The disturbances of which we have knowledge were in fact mainly in the west of Scotland, where there was trouble involving the Lord of Lorne and the Earl of Argyll, and in the north, where the Earl of Ross (who was also Lord of the Isles) appropriated crown revenues and raided the properties of the Earl of Orkney. Obviously, there were those who were ready to seize any opportunity for the pursuit of their private ends by violent means, and the lesson was one of the weakness of the executive machine. The strong hand of an active monarch was necessary if government was to be carried on successfully.

On the other hand, the unexpected death of one King and the accession of another, only nine years of age, did not destroy continuity of policy, for the siege of Roxburgh Castle was pressed to a successful conclusion and two days after it fell the new King was crowned in the nearby Abbey of Kelso, only some five miles from the English frontier. Once more, as after the death of James I, the resolution of the Queen Mother to meet the challenge and continue her husband's policy may well have helped to shape the situation. It was to Mary of Gueldres, along with a council of regency, that the conduct of affairs and the custody of the King were officially entrusted. There was some criticism of her participation in the administration, but the new government gained a fortuitous success in foreign policy which greatly strengthened its position. In the civil war which was going on in England between York and Lancaster, the Scottish government on the whole tended to favour Lancaster (whereas the Earl of Douglas, it will be recalled, had allied with York). At this stage Margaret of Anjou, the determined wife of the Lancastrian Henry VI, came to Scotland to seek help, and then, after a fresh Lancastrian effort had been defeated at Towton (1461), Margaret and Henry visited Scotland together and ceded Berwick to the Scots in return for a promise of assistance. The acquisition first of Roxburgh and then of the great prize of Berwick was enough to bring about a large measure of agreement in Scotland to support the council of regency.

But the policy of intervening in the affairs of a neighbouring country was a game at which two could play. Edward IV, who had become King of England at the expense of Henry VI, retaliated against the Scottish support of Lancaster by cultivating the exiled Earl of Douglas and also the Lord of the Isles, who was showing little disposition to acknowledge the government being carried on in the name of James III. With these Scottish malcontents Edward made in 1462 an agreement which has been called the Treaty of Westminster-Ardtornish (for Ardtornish Castle, on the Sound of Mull, was a seat of the Lord of the Isles). By this treaty, the rulers of the Isles, in return for pensions from England, were to become the liegemen of the King of England and to support him in his wars against the King of Scots; and, in the event of the conquest of Scotland by England with the assistance of Douglas and the Lord of the Isles, Scotland north of the Forth was to be partitioned between the two Scottish traitors. It is unlikely that Edward IV seriously thought that he could succeed in doing something which the three previous Edwards had failed to do, but the agreement was put into effect to the extent that action was taken which embarrassed the Scottish government and reduced the likelihood that it would render effective help to Henry VI. The Lord of the Isles, from his headquarters at Inverness, assumed sovereign powers and arrogated to himself the prerogatives of royalty. When he was summoned to compear before parliament, it is hardly surprising that he 'comperit nocht'. In the south, Douglas reappeared in Scotland, with English backing. He had little success, but the difficulties created for the Scottish government had the result (which Edward desired) of stimulating the Scots to reconsider the question of their relations with the English government.

It is creditable to the intelligence of Mary of Gueldres that she seems to have been one of the first to see that Douglas and the Lord of the Isles might be neutralised if Scotland came to terms with Edward IV and abandoned what now seemed to be the lost cause of Lancaster. But, while she carried 'the young lords' with her, 'the old lords', guided by Bishop Kennedy of St Andrews, adhered to the policy of favouring Lancaster. Mary did her cause no good by entering into an association with Hepburn of Hailes and trying, along with him, to gain control of the young King's person. When she was thus discredited, in much the same way as Joan Beaufort had been by her marriage with Stewart of Lorne, the leading position in the administration fell to Bishop Kennedy. He found, however, that he had to turn to Mary's policy to the extent of coming to terms with Edward IV. There was therefore no fresh incursion by Douglas, and the Lord of the Isles returned to his allegiance, on the occasion of a progress by the twelve-year-old King to Inverness and Moray in August 1464. The Queen Mother had died in December 1463.

The death of Kennedy in 1465, after a period of stability which had been all too brief, left a gap which there was no statesman to fill, and out of a confused and uncertain situation there emerged the ascendancy of the Boyds—an episode curiously parallel to that of the Livingstons with which the minority of James II closed. Early in 1466 Sir Alexander Boyd, the brother of Robert, Lord Boyd of Kilmarnock, entered into a league or bond with Robert, Lord Fleming, and Gilbert, Lord Kennedy. They were not newcomers to office or influence, for Boyd was governor of Edinburgh Castle and military instructor to the young King, Fleming had been steward of the household under James II and Kennedy was the brother of the late Bishop. They had this also in common, that their power and family connections all lay in the south-western quarter of the country, but with those ringleaders there were associated some other notables—Montgomery, Hamilton, Somerville, Hepburn of Hailes, Ker of Cesford, and Crawford. By the terms of their agreement, Kennedy and Boyd were to have the King in their hands, while Fleming was to be compensated with money or lands. In July 1466 the King was seized by Boyd and Fleming at Linlithgow and carried off to Edinburgh Castle. At a meeting of parliament in October, Lord Boyd obtained from the fourteen-year-old King a solemn statement that the conspirators had acted in accordance with the royal wishes, and Boyd was officially appointed guardian of the King and his brothers.

Although Lord Boyd became chamberlain in 1467, the Boyd 'kin' did not engross office as the Livingstons had done, and were possibly more interested in influence and profit. It was Thomas Boyd, the eldest son of Lord Boyd, who became the leading man in the country. In 1467 he married the King's sister, Mary, with a dowry of 1,000 merks, he was created Earl of Arran, he received estates in Ayrshire and elsewhere and he was appointed sheriff of Arran and Wigtown and steward of Kirkcudbright. But he made many enemies, and when he went overseas in 1468, on an embassy to arrange for the King's marriage, his enemies seized their opportunity to bring about the ruin of his house, although he himself escaped by returning to the Continent. Sir Alexander Boyd was beheaded in November 1469, his brother and his nephew were forfeited and their possessions annexed to the crown.

The marriage of James III was an event of unusual, and in some ways unique, significance. He commissioned envoys to travel widely on the Continent to look for an eligible princess, and it is related that they found no bride so suitable as Margaret, the daughter of King Christian I of Denmark and Norway. Her father undertook to give her a dowry of 60,000 florins of the Rhine, but an agreement was reached in 1468 that, pending the payment of the full amount, Christian would pay 10,000 florins and pledge his lands and rights in Orkney in security for the remainder. The treaty telling the whole story is still to be seen in the Register House at Edinburgh. However, when the time came for Christian to put down the 10,000 florins, he found that he could raise only 2,000 florins, and in 1469 he therefore entered on a further pledge, now of his property in Shetland. Orkney and Shetland had by this time been in Norwegian occupation for some six centuries or more, and had never formed part of the Scottish realm, but Scottish infiltration into Orkney had been going on for some years. Most of the lands and revenues of the islands belonged not to the crown of Norway and Denmark but to the earldom of Orkney, which since 1379 had been held by the Scottish family of St Clair. In 1470 James III came to an agreement with the Earl of Orkney whereby the latter received lands in Fife in exchange for his properties in the north. Thus, after the rights of the Norwegian crown in the islands had passed to the Scottish crown in pledge, the earldom of Orkney and lordship of Shetland passed to it in property.

The pledge by the King of Denmark was never redeemed, though his successors frequently tried to open negotiations for the redemption of their rights, and the upshot was that the islands remained Scottish possessions. James III's marriage thus brought the Scottish kingdom at last to its full geographical extent.

The marriage of James to Margaret of Denmark took place at Holyrood on 13 July 1469. Their family consisted of three sons—James, born on 17 March 1473, who succeeded as James IV; another James, born in March 1476, who was created Duke of Ross in 1488 and died in January 1503; and John, born in December 1479, who was created Earl of Mar in 1486 and died on 11 March 1503.

As had happened with James II, the marriage of James III marks the point at which the minority came to an end. The family which had established its ascendancy—this time the Boyds—was disposed of and the King began to exercise his personal influence on the course of events. The traditional picture of this King's character and its effect on affairs is clear-cut, but has been repeated generation by generation without receiving much critical examination. The picture is one of a king given over to the company of low-born favourites—a musician, a tailor and a shoemaker among others—and unfit, by his tastes and his temperament, to act as a military leader or to face with resolution the task of governing Scotland. Preferring the company of his favourites, he neglected the nobility. It is also alleged that he was shifty, unstable and perhaps treacherous in his dealings with his brothers, brothers who possessed the qualities of energy, leadership and ability which the King lacked but which appealed to the Scottish people. For reasons which cannot even be guessed at, James caused one brother, the Earl of Mar, to be confined in Craigmillar Castle, and the other, the Duke of Albany, in Edinburgh Castle. Mar, after being removed from Craigmillar to a house in the Canongate, died in captivity, and some believed that he had been murdered at the King's command, but Albany escaped, to be taken up by Edward IV as 'Alexander IV', a vassal-pretender to the Scottish crown. In 1482 an English army, accompanied not only by Albany but also by Edward IV's old Scottish ally, the Earl of Douglas, moved against Scotland, and James reluctantly gathered an army to meet it. At Lauder his disgruntled nobles, irked by James's neglect of their company and advice and by his elevation of his favourite, Cochrane, to the earldom of Mar, took advantage of the situation to press demands for the withdrawal of debased money and the surrender of the favourites; only on such conditions, they said, would they follow the King. A picturesque story relates that most of the nobles were too timid to face the King with their ultimatum, and found themselves in the position of the mice who agreed that it would be to their advantage should one of them hang a bell round the cat's neck, if only a mouse could be found to do so—whereupon Archibald, Earl of Angus, declared, 'I will bell the cat'. On James's refusal to agree to their terms, the nobles seized the favourites, hanged them over the bridge at Lauder and confined the King in Edinburgh Castle.

The English, faced with a divided enemy, were able to appropriate Berwick, which this time they retained permanently. Albany came to terms with some of the Scots lords on the understanding that he would remain faithful to King James, and this led to his being made lieutenant of the kingdom of Scotland. But, at the same time, he was assuring the English that nothing he undertook in Scotland would interfere with his treaty with England and his determination to win the crown of Scotland for himself. Then, possibly because his treachery was discovered, he was relieved of his office of lieutenant in the spring of 1483, the King recovered his authority and an armed incursion from England by Albany and Douglas was defeated in 1484. Douglas was captured and confined, Albany escaped to France, where he was killed a year later. The King was thus confirmed in control of affairs, but he continued to neglect the nobles, he accumulated a treasure in a 'black box' in Stirling Castle and, after the death of the Queen on 14 July 1486, he lived a secluded life in Stirling. At the beginning of 1488 a confederacy of nobles secured the person of the heir apparent and challenged the King in the field. After a skirmish at Blackness in May, a truce was patched up, and the King disbanded his forces, but he was soon faced by another muster of the disaffected faction and encountered them at Sauchieburn, near Stirling, on 11 June. As James fled from the field, or was carried off by his horse, he was thrown to the ground. Asked his identity by a woman drawing water from a well nearby, he replied, 'I was your King this day at morn', and, carried into a cottage, asked for a priest. The woman ran out, crying, 'A priest, a priest for the King'. A passer-by whose identity has never been discovered claimed to be a priest and, introduced to the King, stabbed him to death.

Such is the traditional story, but the truth is probably much more complex. If we had more evidence, it might emerge that this King was a man in advance of his time and possessed of considerable shrewdness of judgment, but that circumstances, in the Scotland of his day, were too strong for him. There can be little doubt, at any rate, that James was a man of artistic and cultured interests. Among his alleged favourites, those for whom it is perhaps least possible to offer a defence were Hommyl, a tailor, and Leonard, a shoemaker; but even in relation to them we have to remember that it was a time when men of substance spent vast sums on their personal adornment, and James may have shown his good taste in his clothing as in other things. It hardly fits in with the picture of James as inactive and timid that another of the favourites was Torphichen, a swordsman; this suggests that James had not entirely forgotten his early training in military exercises by Sir Alexander Boyd. Another favourite was John Ireland, a learned doctor of the Sorbonne, who in 1483 returned to settle in his native Scotland and became the King's confessor. Robert Cochrane, contemptuously referred to by the nobles as a stonemason, was in fact an architect, and the patronage of such a man can hardly be considered reprehensible, especially as the age was one when many buildings of high quality were being erected in Scotland. Another of the favourites was Rogers, an Englishman, contemptuously called a fiddler, but more likely an accomplished musician, and this again connects with one of the notable developments of the time, for one of the objects of the collegiate churches which had become so fashionable was to render divine service with choral and instrumental music impossible in the ordinary parish church. We know, besides, that James sent a 'lutar', or lute-player, overseas to learn his craft and that he presented an organ to the collegiate church of the Holy Trinity which his mother had founded in Edinburgh. It should not be forgotten, either, that James was devout in his religious observance, especially in his later years, and that his Queen, Margaret of Denmark, was a woman of such outstanding piety that she was put forward as a candidate for canonisation. James was very likely a patron of painting as well as of architecture and music, and certainly the oldest pieces of first-rate painting extant in Scotland date from his reign: one depicted the King with a young prince, another depicted the Queen, and they were formerly part of an altar-piece in that same royal foundation of Trinity College. It is significant of the influx of artistic concepts from the Continent that a groat of James III (1485) is claimed to bear the earliest Renaissance coin portrait found outside Italy.

It may seem less creditable to James that he took an interest in astrology, but in those days astrology comprehended not only fortune-telling by the stars but also what we now know as the respectable science of astronomy. And it is very likely that his interests extended to other branches of science. Some of the payments so frequently recorded to the King's physicians may indicate not that he suffered from ill health but that he was interested in medicine. It is certainly significant that one of the men of low degree whom he raised to high office was William Scheves, who started his career as the royal physician. Scheves was a scholar and lover of books, and some of the richly bound volumes which once adorned his library still survive. He was noted also as an astrologer or astronomer, and a treatise on an eclipse of the sun, written in the Low Countries, was dedicated to him. Such was the background of the man who was promoted by James III to the archbishopric of St Andrews. It was something of a surprise appointment, for both his immediate predecessors had been men of noble family, and indeed of royal descent, whereas Scheves, by contrast, was the complete parvenu.

There is some evidence that James III's reign saw a flowering of literature. The best poet of the day whose writings have survived was William Henryson, but we know of others by their reputations if not by their extant works. In a poem written in the next reign, William Dunbar mentions by name a great many poets who had preceded him and who were now dead: the catalogue is punctuated by the refrain, *Timor mortis conturbat me*. Admittedly, some of those deceased poets belonged to still earlier periods, but the majority of them must have flourished under James III, and some of them are mentioned in the Treasurer's Accounts as having received pensions from the King.

Creditable as is James III's patronage of learning and the arts, it would probably be more impressive if we had more evidence. In particular, the Treasurer's Accounts, which detail matters like pensions to poets and payments to craftsmen, are extant for only a year or so of James III's reign. The fact that this particular record suddenly becomes more copious and continuous in the reign of

James IV gives that monarch a great advantage over his predecessors and has led to the attribution to his reign of the beginnings of developments which had actually started earlier. This point can be illustrated in maritime history. We hear much in James IV's reign of the exploits of his sea-captains and of the courage with which they engaged their ships in battle. But the ship *The Yellow Carvel*, which became famous in James IV's reign, was apparently previously owned by James III and appears on record in 1474. Moreover, Sir Andrew Wood, renowned as a captain under James IV, was employed by James III, and, loyal to him to the end, was in command of the royal ships in 1488 at the time of the Sauchieburn campaign. So it would seem that in his interest in naval matters, as in so much else, James III may have anticipated his son.

As for James III's brothers, with whom he is so often compared to his disadvantage, we know far too little to be able to speak with any confidence. Mar, in fact, is no more than a name. About Albany we have more information, but it is hard to believe that anyone would seriously defend a man who seems to have been moved only by ambition and who was prepared to accept the Scottish crown at the hands of the English King. The fairest comment on James III's relations with Mar and Albany may be simply that it was his misfortune to have brothers of mature years. It was unusual in the history of the Stewart dynasty, for James's case is almost the only one between the reign of Robert III and that of Charles II. Robert III had had troubles enough with his brother, the Governor Albany; since then, James I and James II had been the only surviving sons of their fathers; and when we come to James IV, who had a brother, we find that he sought to neutralise any potential rivalry by making him an archbishop. James V, Mary, James VI and Charles I were again free from the possible challenge of a brother. It fell to James III to cope with this unusual liability as best he could.

James's misfortunes can hardly be explained by constitutional irresolution. He showed decision enough when he arrested Mar and Albany, and it was just bad luck for him that Albany escaped.

Equally, James's actions after Albany established his ascendancy in 1482 were not discreditable. It is true that Albany's own record was not distinguished by statesmanship, and he probably suffered in prestige because he came in company with an English army, so that he may have been driven to reach an accommodation with the King in the hope of being able to use him as a figurehead. But James set himself to undermine Albany's position, with the result that Albany was soon thrown back on Edward of England, with whom he renewed his compact in 1483. Then, evidently because the King's stock was rising while Albany's was falling, the latter resigned the office of lieutenant of the kingdom and returned to England. It was then a good stroke of fortune for James that Edward IV died (1483), leaving Albany without an assured future south of the Border and cutting the ground from him. He was forfeited by the Scottish parliament in 1483. James continued to show spirit and resolution enough for a time thereafter, and if he was vacillating and irresolute in the final months of his reign, before Sauchieburn, the reason may have been that he wanted if possible to save his country from the miseries of civil war.

When we look beyond personalities for the deeper causes of the difficulties of this reign, it emerges that a rapidly changing economic situation may have been part of the explanation. The period was one of very considerable prosperity. There had been comparative freedom from serious invasions for some time, and the southern parts of the country, naturally the most fertile and productive, were able to recover from the effects of war and to play their rightful part in the national economy. It was no accident that it was under James II that Edinburgh had first begun to have the semblance of a capital: it was the place of that King's birth, coronation, marriage and burial, and it became the normal meeting place of the exchequer. James III acknowledged its position when he gave the town formal recognition as his capital. It is probably indicative of a general increase in prosperity that the second half of the fifteenth century saw the foundation of a number of burghs of barony, in which crafts could be exercised and internal trade conducted but which (unlike the privileged royal burghs) had no share in foreign trade. The growing wealth of Scotland is reflected also in somewhat lavish expenditure on buildings, especially churches. Among royal foundations, the most notable was Trinity College, Edinburgh, founded by James III's mother in his minority, but James himself was interested in the collegiate churches of Restalrig and Tain. Of the many collegiate churches on which noblemen expended their substance the most conspicuous example is Rosslyn Chapel, which displays a riot of decoration achieved at enormous cost. Large and fine churches in towns were equally eloquent of the wealth of the burgesses; among examples still to be seen are the Holy Rude at Stirling and St Michael's at Linlithgow. Secular building is less well documented than churches, and less of it has survived, but there was evidence of royal building at the palaces of Linlithgow and Stirling (where there was a great hall, attributed, without proof, to Cochrane) and in the 'King's Wark' at Leith.

But the real wealth which those buildings represent, and the obvious desire to spend, were accompanied by a great scarcity of bullion and consequently by monetary difficulties; for years the Scottish parliament was much occupied with 'the matter of the money'. Possibly out of a sincere desire to meet a real need, possibly from less reputable motives, changes were made in the coinage. New copper farthings made their appearance, ostensibly at least 'for the eise and sustentatioun of the Kingis liegis and almous deid to be done to pur folk'—that is, to facilitate the giving of alms to the poor—and this rather suggests that the existing coins were out of line with real values. There was also debasement of the coinage, for which Cochrane, the King's architect friend, was blamed. And it is a curious, and probably significant, fact that King James himself amassed a very considerable personal treasure in gold and silver. A sixteenth-century writer describes him as 'wondrous covetous', and there was a good deal of talk about his 'black box' in Stirling Castle. If, at a time of shortage of coin, the King was engrossing an unduly high proportion of the available bullion, and withdrawing it from circulation, this would not add to his popularity. It is an interesting commentary on the proceedings of this reign that at the beginning of the next a statute declared that 'a trew substantious man' should be in charge of the mint, to prevent tampering with the coin. Even so, however much James's policy was disliked by the nobles, it can hardly be contended that he was unpopular with the commons, for he had substantial support from the burgesses at the end of his reign, and three years after his death there was still a 'heavy murmur and voice of the people' because his murderers had not been brought to justice. A sixteenth-century writer says that he was well beloved by all the commons and burghs.

Possibly yet another reason for James III's difficulties lay in his display of anglophile tendencies. He showed a marked reluctance to lead armies against the English, even when the English King was the Yorkist Edward IV, with his record of supporting Scottish rebels. In 1480, it was only pressure from Louis XI of France which led him to go to war with England, and the army that advanced to the Border was not led by the King in person. Then, when the English retaliated by sending a fleet which did a good deal of damage in the Firth of Forth area in 1481, James, under this provocation, did consent to lead an army against England, but was prevailed on to turn back by a message from a papal envoy which threatened him with interdict if he proceeded. James was also always interested in English marriage projects. He pursued schemes for intermarriage with the English royal family with the utmost pertinacity, though in the end with no success. In 1474 there were plans for a marriage between Cecilia, youngest daughter of Edward IV, and Prince James, the heir to the Scottish throne. In 1477 it was proposed that James's sister, Margaret, should marry the Duke of Clarence, Edward IV's brother, and in 1478 that she should marry Earl Rivers, one of Edward's closest supporters. In 1484 a niece of Richard III was proposed as the bride of Prince James. Then, after the death of Queen Margaret in 1486, James entered into negotiations for his own marriage to the widow of Edward IV and for the marriage of two of his sons to daughters of Edward IV. After Richard III was superseded by Henry VII, James opened negotiations with him, and it was proposed that the two kings should meet in July 1488. English brides for Scottish Kings, though common enough in the days before the War of Independence—indeed almost the invariable practice for two centuries—had been rare since the War of Independence. David II had married Joanna under the terms of the Treaty of Northampton, and James I had brought back his bride with him from his English captivity. But David II's second marriage and the marriages of Robert II and Robert III had been to Scotswomen, while James II and James III had both found their wives on the Continent.

Scottish bitterness against England, which had been persistent for over a century, was at this time excited by the destruction caused by the armies of 'the reiver Edward, calling himself King of England', and the verses of Blind Harry were recalling to the minds of Scotsmen the deeds of William Wallace, in lines coloured by the strongest hatred of the English. In such a climate of opinion, James III's anglophile policy was bound to arouse suspicion. One of the counts against him was that his counsellors advised him 'to the inbringing of Englishmen and to the perpetual subjection of the realm'. No doubt this was a good propaganda description of James's efforts for peace and marriages, and the fact that his opponents, at the end of his reign, themselves made overtures to Henry VII suggests that the criticism of his anglophile policy was a mere pretence. At the same time, there is evidence that one of James's favourites, John Ramsay, whom he created Lord of Bothwell, was an active English agent. Yet it may be that in his foreign policy, as in much else, James III was ahead of his time. It was not unstatesmanlike to discern the folly of continued hostility to England or to neutralise Albany and other malcontents by conciliating the power which might assist them. And James's matrimonial quests came to fruition under his son, who married Margaret Tudor.

The final crisis of this reign emerged from the policy which James followed after he had ousted Albany and recovered his authority in 1483. For a time the King seems to have acted not with too little resolution, but with rather too much resolution. In 1484, at his instance, parliament proceeded against the supporters of Albany by forfeiting Lord Crichton and about thirty others. This sweeping action, which to some extent recalls those of James I and anticipates those of James V, may, by creating a powerful band of dispossessed barons, have contributed to the fall of James III. At this stage there was also an act suspending for a year the granting of remissions and respites for treason and other offences, indicating that there was now to be a firmer policy.

It may be, however, that James did not maintain his resolution and was not consistent enough in energy or steadily active in administration. Very possibly he lacked interest in the tasks of government, and, despite an occasional phase of severity, he was on the whole mild and merciful, too ready to excuse and pardon offences. On two occasions in earlier years parliament had reproached him for his slackness in executing the law and his readiness to grant remissions and respites. It may well be true that after the Queen's death in 1486 he lived a retired life, and he continued to neglect those who regarded themselves as his natural councillors, preferring churchmen, officials and new peers, rather than peers of older standing. It has been suggested that his preference for the company and advice of 'new men' issued in a novel emphasis during his reign on the council, the membership of which was at least partly in the King's choice, rather than on the parliament, where the great men were so firmly entrenched. There is little real evidence of this, just as there is no real evidence that Cochrane had ever been created Earl of Mar. Yet, while James did not, so far as we know, admit his low-born favourites to political responsibility, he may have consulted them informally and attached more importance to their views than to those of the nobles. If there is anything in this, then the King's neglect of his nobles as councillors would aggravate the discontent caused by his devotion to artists and craftsmen.

The events which brought discontent to a head reflected some of the royal tastes which had led to criticism of James in earlier years. At this point, his career, and the cause of his misfortunes, anticipate those of his descendant Charles I, another king who was a patron of the arts. Charles had as the centre of his policy the intention of recovering for the Church the property which had belonged to it earlier and ensuring that it was adequately endowed, and it was largely because he threatened to deprive the Scottish nobles of their church lands that he came to grief. Now James, it has been observed, was also a devout monarch; and his reign was one in which there was a great development of collegiate churches, in which he was interested. On the other hand, monasteries were coming to be regarded as rather out of date, and no one took very seriously their claim to be a worth-while part of the Church. James therefore proposed that to his chapel royal there should be annexed half of the revenues of the priory of Coldingham, a Benedictine house which was in decay both materially and spiritually. But the revenues of Coldingham were in effect in the hands of the powerful Border family of Home, and the Homes allied with another powerful house, that of Hepburn, against the King. The parliament of January 1488 decreed that action should be taken against all who opposed the transfer of revenues from Coldingham. This brought on the crisis, for a strong coalition of lords was formed against the King, including magnates like the Earl of Angus as well as Home and Hepburn of Hailes, and they managed to secure the person of Prince James, the heir apparent.

The crown's struggle with its rivals had been taking on a new character in this reign, and the novelty emerged with peculiar clarity in the last months. Under James III there had been no great combinations of barons with rather nebulous aims. The object of the opposition appears now to have been the attainment of influence over the crown; it almost appears that the barons, faced by a monarchy becoming ever stronger, sought not to overthrow it, but to control it. The reason for the change may be sought partly in the increasing wealth of the crown, which explains why no subject now attained a position such as Douglas had held under James II and why no other family could now hope either to replace the Stewarts or become independent of them.

The crown was now far superior in wealth to even the greatest of the nobles, and it may therefore have seemed a more profitable policy to control the crown, which enjoyed so much landed wealth and the influence which went with it, rather than to take action which would lead to the dissipation of its resources. For this reason, the opposition under James III attacked not the crown, or even the ruling line, but the person of the King. They concentrated on the alleged weaknesses of James's character and capabilities, and turned to another member of the ruling line—first James's brother, the Duke of Albany, later Prince James. The criticisms of James, sometimes for his 'low favourites', sometimes for his supposed pro-English policy, were perhaps chiefly mere excuses, or a device to justify the baronial policy to the mass of the people. Besides, the baronage was far from united. There had been conspicuous signs even under James II that the crown could count on some noble families against others, and James III was even more successful in retaining the support of some of the leading men. In 1476 he had the support of the Earl of Crawford, the representative of a family so hostile to his father. There are indications that as the crisis of 1488 approached James imitated his father by ennobling men who would support him: four lords of parliament—Crichton of Sanquhar, Ruthven, Drummond and Sempill—were created at the beginning of the year, and in May Lord Kilmaurs was promoted to the earldom of Glencairn and the Earl of Crawford was created Duke of Montrose. In the actual campaign, most of the magnates of the north and north-east of the country rallied to the King—men like Huntly, Errol, Atholl and Marischal; this situation anticipates one which was to recur frequently in later centuries, when the more loyal, or more conservative, northern nobles were again and again to be found on the side of the house of Stewart against its enemies. Nor was support for James III confined to such magnates, for he continued to have the countenance of the wise and good Bishop Elphinstone of Aberdeen, as well as his personal friend and old crony Scheves of St Andrews (while the Bishop of Glasgow, the jealous rival of Scheves, naturally took the other side). All in all, the opposition

6 The inauguration of Alexander III

From a fifteenth-century MS. of Fordun's 'Scotichronicon' (Corpus Christi College, Cambridge MS. 171, f.205a)

7 David I and Malcolm IV
From a contemporary Charter in the National Library of Scotland

8 – 9 The Seal of the Guardians, 1286: obverse and reverse
(British Museum)

10 Dunfermline: the largely rebuilt Norman Abbey can be seen behind the ruins of the Palace of James VI

11 Rothesay Castle in the Isle of Bute, completed in the later thirteenth century

12 Linlithgow Palace and St Michael's Church, West Lothian, mainly of the fifteenth century

Jacob von gots
genaden kůng
von schottland

13 James II

From an illumination by Jörg von Ehingen
(Landesbibliothek, Stuttgart Cod. Hist. 4° 141)

14 James III

15 Queen Margaret

16 James IV and Queen Margaret
From the Seton Armorial, c. 1600

17 James IV, with his hawk

Both from contemporary paintings

18 Queen Margaret depicted with symbolism which hints at her unstable affections. The man on the left may be either Angus or Albany

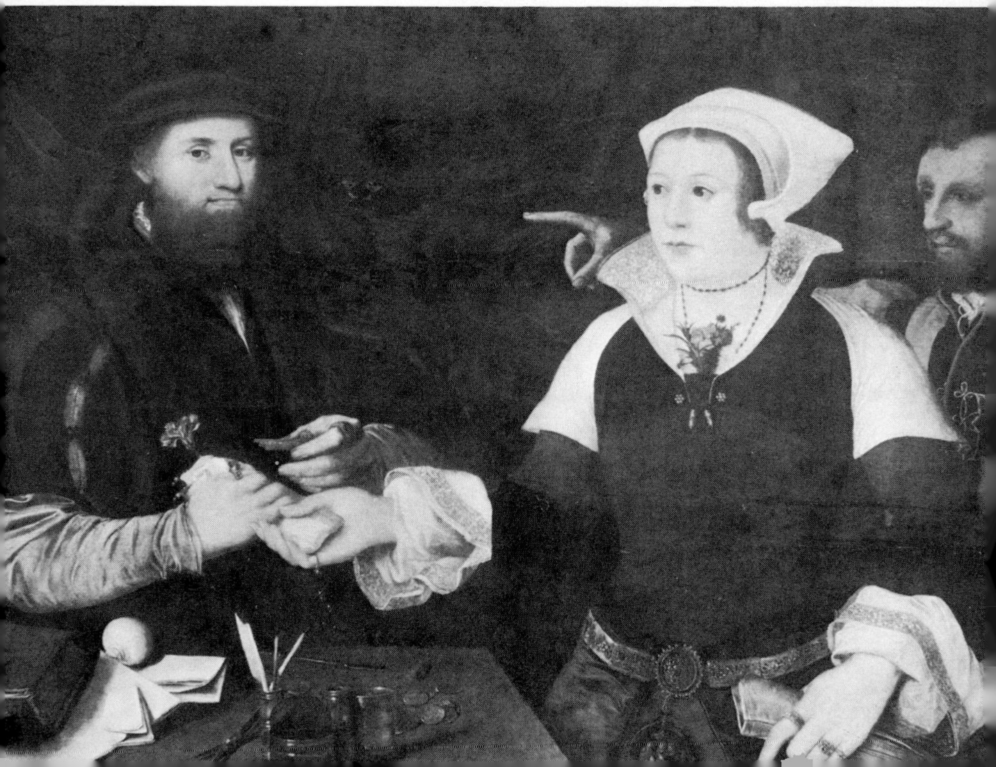

19 James V and his first wife Madeleine
From the Seton Armorial, c. 1600

20 The Renaissance Palace at Stirling Castle, 1540-2

ROYAL WORKS DURING THE REIGN OF JAMES V

21 Falkland Palace, Fife: the gateway of c. 1500 and the new south façade, 1537-41

22 James V

From a contemporary portrait by an unknown artist

23 Mary of Guise-Lorraine, second wife of James V

From a contemporary portrait by an unknown artist

24 A 'Stirling head', possibly James V
Wooden medallion from Stirling Castle

25 Mary, Queen of Scots
From a sketch by François Clouet

26 James VI (left), with his grandparents the Earl and Countess of Lennox and his uncle Charles, prays for vengeance on the murderers of his father, Henry, Lord Darnley

From Livinius de Vogelaare, 'Memorial to Lord Darnley'

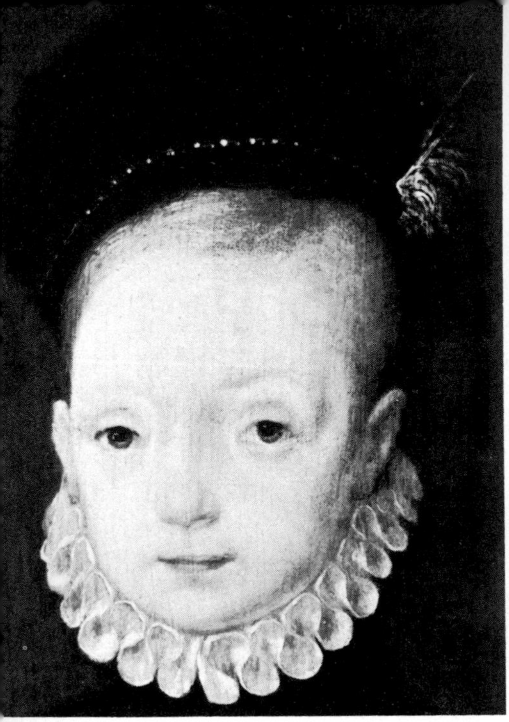

27 James VI as a boy

28 James Stewart, Earl of Moray

THE YOUNG KING AND HIS REGENTS

29 James Douglas, Earl of Morton

30 John, Earl of Mar

31 James VI as a young man of 29

From a portrait painted in 1595

32 James VI in middle age

From a miniature by Isaac Oliver

now looks like a mere party or faction, and a royal party has clearly become a strong element in the situation.

Never again after Sauchieburn was a Scottish King to encounter in the field a resolute combination of his subjects in arms; never again, as long as Scotland remained an independent kingdom, was a Scottish monarch to be defeated by his subjects in the field. Besides, while the insurgents may well have been disposed to supersede James by his son and heir as the tool of their own faction, there is no evidence that they premeditated the killing of the King. The murder of James as he fled from the field of Sauchieburn was a hole-and-corner affair, and not a public demonstration. It was, indeed, in the nature of a fatal accident, and it was not inappropriate that the records of parliament refer to it as such—the 'unhappy field' of Sauchieburn, 'in the quhilk the King our soverane lord happinit to be slane'.

33 Linlithgow Palace
From John Slezer, 'Theatrum Scotiae'

7

A Popular Hero: James IV, 1488-1513

It seemed for a brief space after the accession of James IV that an old pattern was going to be repeated, to the extent that just as Livingstons had risen in the minority of James II and Boyds in that of James III, so now the families of Home and Hepburn, who had been mainly responsible for the overthrow of the late King, would establish a domination. They did indeed profit largely. Lord Home became great chamberlain, warden of the east marches, bailie of Ettrick Forest, keeper of the castles of Newark and Stirling, steward of the earldom of Mar and custodian of one of the King's brothers. Lord Hailes, head of the house of Hepburn, became master of the household, constable of Edinburgh Castle, warden of the west and middle marches, high admiral and custodian of another of the King's brothers, and a little later he was promoted to the earldom of Bothwell and put into possession of Liddesdale. Another Hepburn was keeper of the privy seal, and yet another was clerk of the rolls, register and council.

It also seemed obvious that, while the victors enjoyed their rewards, a government which had come into being as a result of a successful insurrection could hardly expect from the outset to command universal support throughout the country. It may be significant of a desire to omit nothing which might legalise the revolution that James IV, unlike his father and grandfather, was crowned at Scone, where no later King save Charles II was to be crowned. If this was merely politic, there were soon signs of statesmanship, in what looks like a policy of appeasement all round. For example, it was ordained that the heirs of those who had been killed when fighting on the losing side at Sauchieburn should succeed to their fathers' estates as if their fathers had died 'at the faith and peace of our sovereign lord the King'. And, when the Earl of Lennox and Lord Lyle raised a rebellion in 1489, although energetic action was taken against them and the royal artillery speedily compelled the surrender of their castles, their forfeitures were soon rescinded and a pardon granted to their supporters.

Besides, any resemblance of the situation after James IV's accession to that in the minorities of his three predecessors was bound to be short-lived at the best, for this time there was hardly a minority at all. James had the advantage over most of the kings of his house in that he started his reign at the age of nearly sixteen, which, by Stewart standards, meant mature years; indeed, already on his accession he was half as old as James II and James V were when they died. His reign is therefore an uncommonly long period—twenty-five years—of personal rule by an able king; the longest period of that kind in Scottish history between the reign of Alexander III and that of James VI.

A description of James IV comes to us from a Spanish visitor to Scotland, Pedro de Ayala. According to this flattering contemporary, James was 'of noble stature, neither tall nor short, and as handome in complexion and shape as a man can be. . . . He speaks the following foreign languages: Latin, very well; French, German, Flemish, Italian and Spanish. . . . He is courageous, even more so than a king should be.' James, we know from other sources, was an intelligent man with many and varied interests and an enquiring turn of mind particularly suited to a period when geographical discovery and developments in arts of every kind were immensely widening men's horizons. One of his hobbies was medicine and 'surgery', for he took an interest in surgical operations and patronised 'leeches' more actively than his father had done. When he himself had to be 'bled', the surgeon's fee was 28*s*., but James was quite willing to pay the same amount to one of his subjects 'to give the King leave to let him blood'. He experimented likewise in dentistry, for he paid 14*s*. to 'ane fallow, because the King pullit furth his teeth', and another 14*s*. to one of his own barber-surgeons for the privilege of drawing two of the latter's teeth.

The King's most celebrated leech was the Italian, or possibly French, Damian, whom he appointed to the abbey of Tongland and whose chief claim to notoriety was his manufacture of a pair of wings with which he took off from the ramparts of Stirling Castle, only to come to grief on the rocks below. Damian was also an alchemist, and the King encouraged him in his experiments, at least so far as they seemed likely to lead to the transmutation of lead into gold. But the King's interest in the sciences bore more important fruit than his patronage of poor Damian, for in this reign there was founded King's College, Aberdeen, the first university in Great Britain to have a foundation for the teaching of medicine, and in 1506 the Royal College of Surgeons of Edinburgh received its charter from James IV.

Concern for education extended beyond the faculty of medicine. To the year 1496 there belongs a statute which is claimed to be the first compulsory education act: all barons and freeholders of substance were ordered to 'put thair eldest sonnis and airis to the sculis fra thai be aucht or nine yeiris of age and till remane at the grammer sculis quhill [until] thai . . . have perfite Latyne'. In 1512 a new college—St Leonard's—was founded at the University of St Andrews by Prior John Hepburn. The King's more personal interest in education is shown in the care he took of the schooling of his illegitimate sons, Alexander and James. Alexander was sent to Italy in 1507 and spent three years there. He was first at Padua, where his brother later joined him, and the boys studied also at Siena and Rome, under the famous scholar, Erasmus, who subsequently wrote a panegyric on Alexander.

The King's interest in literature was reflected in his patronage of poets. William Dunbar, who among other things celebrated the King's marriage in his verses on *The Thistle and the Rose*, constantly complained of neglect, but in spite of—or perhaps because of—his querulousness, he received a pension of £10 a year in 1500, increased in 1507 to £20 and in 1510 to no less than £80, which was a very considerable sum. Besides, James encouraged the printing press, which was introduced to Scotland under royal patronage by Walter Chapman and Andrew Miller, burgesses of Edinburgh, whose earliest productions date from 1508. The poet Dunbar wrote lines which describe the varied interests in arts and crafts of which the royal court was a centre:

Schir, ye have mony servitouris
And officiaris of dyvers curis,
Kirkmen, courtmen and craftismen fyne,
Doctouris in jure and medicyne.
Divinouris, rethoris and philosophouris,
Astrologis, artistis and oratouris,
Men of armes and vailyeant knychtis,
And mony uther gudlie wichtis:
Musicianis, menstralis and mirrie singeris,
Chevalouris, cawanderis and flingaris:
Cunyouris, carvouris and carpentaris, [coiners
Beildaris of barkis and ballingaris: [small ships
Masounis lyand upoun the land
And schipwrichtis hewand upone the strand:
Glasing wrichtis, goldsmithis and lapidaris,
Pryntouris, payntouris and potingaris.

It is true that, thanks to the fact that the Treasurer's Accounts are extant for most of James's reign, we can form a complete picture of his way of life such as we cannot for any earlier monarch. We can trace his pilgrimages and his visits to shrines, with due record of the sums he gave for the celebration of masses or as 'drinksilver' to the builders whom he found at work on churches. Much building was going on at his own residences too: it is in this reign that we first hear of a palace adjoining the old abbey of Holyrood, and some parts of Linlithgow Palace are James IV's work. It was characteristic of his humanity that he gave 14*s.* 'to ane masoun in Faukland that wes pit fra the werk', presumably because he had been injured. We have the record of a payment of two shillings, in 1497, to buy footballs for the King—in defiance of his own statute of six years earlier which had forbidden such unprofitable sport. We see how he moved about the country—partly, as a contemporary remarked, to administer justice and establish order and partly also to consume his revenues in kind—and we glimpse the freedom with which his people approached him: 'to a wife that brocht straberreis to the King . . . to a wife that brocht cherreis to the King and criit on him for silver'. But the mere fact that such records are extant gives James IV an enormous advantage over his predecessors, for whose reigns there is no comparable information, and the creditable figure which James IV cuts is partly an illusion, arising from the dearth of evidence about earlier monarchs.

The flattering De Ayala remarked that 'none of the former Kings have succeeded in bringing the people into such subjection as the present King'. Admittedly, he was writing with special reference to the Highland west, but there is some truth in the statement in relation to the whole country. So far as civil justice is concerned, this reign saw an important stage in the development of a central court. Attempts to secure the administration of civil justice by parliamentary sessions had in the end failed, and recourse to the King-in-council again became so frequent that the councillors alone could not meet the demand. In James IV's reign there appears a conciliar session (consisting of councillors with the addition of others specially qualified as judges), and this was the real beginning of the Court of Session. As to criminal justice, James went assiduously on ayres throughout the country, executing the law 'without respect to rich or poor', and on at least one occasion he led an expedition to the Borders, when many thieves were hanged. He was never lacking in energy.

James's dealings with the Church reflect an outlook which

attached considerable importance to religious observances but would not allow higher considerations to stand in the way of material advantage. On the one hand, therefore, he fostered the order of the Observant Friars, who were the strictest churchmen of the time, and he furthered the endowment of the collegiate churches which had become so fashionable in his father's reign. On the other hand, he initiated the policy, later to be extended by his son, of exploiting his control over the wealthy benefices to the advantage of the crown, and the record of the appointments he made is far from creditable. He passed over a great churchman like Elphinstone, Bishop of Aberdeen, and appointed to the archbishopric of St Andrews first his own brother, James, Duke of Ross, at the age of twenty-one, and then his illegitimate son, Alexander, at the age of eleven. The latter appointment was so startling, even in an age when Rodrigo Borgia had been elevated to the papacy, that James himself admitted Alexander's promotion to be *res sane difficilis vixque speranda*. The Duke of Ross received, in addition to the primacy, the abbeys of Holyrood, Dunfermline and Arbroath, and, while he was maintained on his ecclesiastical revenues, the income from the lands of Ross reverted to the crown. Then, when Alexander was archbishop, the archiepiscopal revenues were paid into the royal treasury. If all this showed no solicitude for the well-being of the Church, it did not indicate solicitude for the well-being of the state either, for Ross, while still under age of twenty-seven, held the office of chancellor of the kingdom, and Alexander was chancellor while still under twenty-one. It does little to palliate the scandal that the pupil of Erasmus, had he lived, might have become an outstanding archbishop.

The flattering statement that no former King had put the people of the Highlands 'under such subjection as the present King' is true to this extent, that James's success was comparative. His achievement was less than is often supposed, and resulted in no permanent changes in the life of the Highlanders or in their relations with the central government. It is true that James was responsible for the final forfeiture of the Lord of the Isles, in

1493, but this raised as many problems as it solved. The various families which had formed a kind of confederacy under the Lord of the Isles were accustomed to act in concert, they were not prepared to acquiesce in the break-up of their organisation, and they were apt to follow any claimant who could make some show of asserting a right to the lapsed lordship. If, in the long run, the traditional organisation was extinguished, that had the effect of removing a focus which might have been one of stability and unity.

How far the forfeiture of the Lord of the Isles in 1493 was from introducing respect for the royal authority was illustrated in the very next year. King James, who had been in Argyll already in 1493, came to the west again in 1494 with a considerable naval force under Sir Andrew Wood, and left a garrison in the castle of Dunaverty, in the district of Kintyre, of which the MacDonalds had been deprived in 1476. James had parted from the main body of his forces, and had himself just set sail from Dunaverty, when the castle was stormed by John MacDonald of Islay and the royal captain of the castle hanged before the very eyes of the outraged King, who was at the time powerless to avenge the insult. James was back in the west again in the following year, and this time he reached Mingary Castle, in Ardnamurchan, where he received the submission of many chiefs and whence he went on to operate in Coll and Tiree. In 1498 he was at the extreme south of Kintyre, in the place now called Campbeltown, and received the homage of more chiefs from the islands. In 1505 he made a progress through the Isles with a great naval force under Sir Andrew Wood and Robert Barton, and the customary submissions came in once more.

However, James could not give the Highlands his undivided attention, and he was therefore obliged to rely on subordinates. In the simpler terms of a purely military problem, he could capture and appropriate castles in the west, but he could not provide royal troops to garrison them. Local magnates, therefore, became captains of castles, and this reign saw the further advancement of two great families, the Campbells of Argyll and the Gordons of

Huntly. Colin Campbell, first Earl of Argyll, received from James IV a grant of lands in Knapdale and the custody of Castle Sween, formerly held by the Lords of the Isles. He also received lands on which to build a castle at Inverlochy, near the modern Fort William. Argyll had already acquired the lordship of Lorne by marriage, and he laid the foundations of a new ascendancy in the west which in time was to be more dangerous to the house of Stewart than the lordship of the Isles had been. While the Campbells thus appeared as King's lieutenants in the south-west, the Gordons appeared as his lieutenants in the north, and the Earl of Huntly became governor of the castle of Inverness. In this reign the family acquired the earldom of Sutherland by marriage and their power and influence extended from Aberdeen to the far north-west. The fortunes were founded also of a third family which much later was almost to rival the Campbells and the Gordons, for Mackenzie of Kintail became deputy governor of the earldom of Ross.

Campbells, Gordons and Mackenzies may have served the King out of a sense of duty, but in serving the King they expected at the same time to advance their own ambitions and the interests of their families at the expense of others. In short, the King was doing no more than exploiting private and family rivalries, so that one family or set of families grew in power while others declined. This laid up trouble for the future. A lieutenant with private ends to serve was not even necessarily interested in the preservation of order, for it was disorder which gave him opportunities of aggrandisement: it was not by keeping the peace that he could earn his reward, but by putting down breakers of the peace, which is not quite the same thing.

At the same time, James saw the desirability of extending a uniform system of administration and justice throughout the kingdom. There was a statute to the effect that the same laws should be administered everywhere, and action was taken to erect additional courts of law in the Highlands. An act of 1504 provided that there should be justices and sheriffs at Inverness or Dingwall for the north and at Tarbert or Campbeltown for the south, and it was also proposed, though nothing came of it, to appoint sheriffs for Ross and Caithness. It is significant, in relation to the concept lying behind the Education Act of 1496, that in this reign one Kenneth Williamson received a grant of land in Skye to support him 'at the schools' so that he might acquire a knowledge of the laws.

During this reign, Scotland's relations with England at first followed a familiar pattern. For one thing, each government intrigued with the disaffected subjects of the other. John Ramsay, who had been a favourite of James III and was dispossessed of his lordship of Bothwell in the new reign, entered into negotiations with Henry VII with a view to kidnapping the King and his brother; and Henry was also in touch with the Earl of Angus, who pledged himself to prevent James from making war on England. James, on his side, took up the cause of Perkin Warbeck, who claimed to be the younger of the two princes of the House of York who had been murdered in the Tower and therefore the rightful possessor of the throne occupied by Henry. Warbeck was welcomed in Scotland and married to a kinswoman of the King, and James conducted campaigns in England on behalf of the pretender. The English government was more anxious for peace than war, and the tale of marriage negotiations between the two royal houses which had characterised the preceding reign went on in this one: at an early stage it was proposed that James should marry Catharine, a cousin of Henry, and Margaret, Henry's daughter, whom James ultimately did marry, was offered to him as early as 1495 when she was only about seven years old.

But it was already apparent in the 1490s that a new international situation was arising in which Scotland might play a part of some consequence. The alliance between Scotland and France was renewed, almost as a matter of course, in 1492, but there were significant negotiations with other continental powers. James offered an alliance to the Emperor Maximilian in joint support of Warbeck. More important, perhaps, were the negotiations with Spain. An embassy came to Scotland from King Ferdinand and

Queen Isabella, the sovereigns of the united Spanish kingdoms, as early as 1489, and a Scottish embassy went to Spain in 1495. The interest of Spain was that Scotland should remain neutral while England, Spain's ally, attacked France. In 1496 and 1497 the Spaniard Pedro de Ayala was twice in Scotland on a mission designed to influence James in the direction of a peaceful policy towards England. It does seem significant that James asked a marriage with a daughter of the Emperor, and, later, a marriage with a daughter of the Spanish sovereigns. He was aiming very high, for his father had been the only Stewart King so far who had married a king's daughter. These were indications—as yet faint indications—that Scottish policy might become part of the pattern of European diplomacy.

But the real change in Scotland's international relations was concerned with Anglo-Scottish policy and came with the turn of the century. Negotiations which had begun in 1498 led in time to a 'treaty of perpetual peace' between England and Scotland in 1502 and to a marriage alliance in 1503—the first real peace between the two countries, as opposed to short-lived truces, since 1332. England and Scotland had been at war, intermittently, since 1296, and the war was to go on, intermittently, until 1560—the Three Hundred Years War. But at this stage, after fully two centuries of Anglo-Scottish warfare, the sixteenth century opened with the promise of better things.

The proposal for a peace cemented by a marriage sprang from the cautious diplomacy of Henry VII, anxious to avoid expensive wars and anxious for security against his ambitious French contemporaries. Henry, of course, was the first Tudor sovereign, whose accession had marked the close of the Wars of the Roses. To establish himself on the throne which he had in fact won by battle on the field of Bosworth, he obtained from parliament not only a declaration of his right but also a petition that he would marry Princess Elizabeth of York, the heiress of the line he had dispossessed. In consenting to that marriage, Henry effected the union of the White Rose with the Red, and his children would represent the competing claims of York and Lancaster. Henry's own experience, within England itself, therefore led him, it has been said, to respect the uses of judicious matrimony, and he proposed to apply the same principle in international relations also. Catharine of Aragon, the daughter of the Spanish sovereigns, was married first to his son Arthur, and then to Arthur's brother, later Henry VIII. It would be an even better stroke for England to secure the friendship of Scotland. The White Rose had been united with the Red; now the Rose was to be united with the Thistle.

And, while in England there was thus a King interested in matrimony as an instrument of diplomacy, in Scotland there was a king in search of a wife—or, to be more precise, James IV was in his later twenties, and his subjects were anxious to see him married. His betrothal to Margaret, daughter of Henry VII, was accordingly arranged. Henry wanted James to accompany his agreement with England with a renunciation of the French alliance, but this James refused. For Scotland to renounce the French alliance would, of course, have meant that she would lose all freedom of action and be in danger of being entirely dominated by England. However, while there was no renunciation of the French alliance, there was a treaty of perpetual peace between Scotland and England, in 1502, and the treaty was strengthened by a papal confirmation, which meant that, should either contracting party be guilty of breaking the engagement, he would incur excommunication.

The marriage of James and Margaret took place at Holyrood on 8 August 1503. They had six children, of whom only one survived infancy. The ultimate result of the marriage, celebrated amid such high hopes, was the union of the crowns exactly a hundred years later, when the great-grandson of James and Margaret, King James VI, became King of England. But the short-term results were less happy. Only ten years after the treaty of perpetual peace, Scotland and England were at war again. Yet the war, when it came, was not of Scotland's making, nor did it arise primarily from Anglo-Scottish relations. It arose from the European situation.

James IV was not averse from foreign adventure. He showed that by sending men and ships to help his uncle, King John of Denmark, against his rebellious subjects in Sweden, and again by sending his sea-captains Robert Barton and Andrew Wood to help King John against Lübeck. He also threatened to intervene in defence of the Duke of Gueldres, to whom likewise he was related by marriage, when that duke was threatened by the Emperor Maximilian. James was, moreover, prepared to support his sea-captains wherever they went and whenever they got into trouble—as they very frequently did, in those days when the partition between lawful trading and piracy was a very thin one.

But, at the same time, James had no wish to see a European war. Indeed, by interest as well as by temperament he was opposed to that, and stood to lose by it, for he was in an awkward position. He was pledged to England by the treaty of perpetual peace which had accompanied his marriage and which was renewed when Henry VIII became King of England in 1509. Because of his loyalty to that treaty, James had declined to make another formal renewal of the league with France, but Scottish opinion urged him to maintain the traditional alliance and from time to time there was pressure from France to remind the Scots of their old association. Plainly, therefore, James could hope to reconcile his legal obligations, to England, with his moral obligations, to France, only as long as England and France did not go to war. He did not want to be in the embarrassing position of having to choose between the two. It has also to be kept in mind that Henry VIII was still childless—Mary, his first child to survive infancy, was not born until 1516—and James's wife was all the time heir presumptive to the English crown; from this point of view peace with England would seem to have been James's interest.

Yet his efforts to preserve, or restore, European peace had another, more disinterested, motive. Although his private life was no model—five illegitimate children, by four different mothers, are recorded—James was dominated by the conventional religious observances of the time. His reign had started as a result of a rebellion which had led to his father's death at Sauchieburn; ever penitent for his part in that rebellion James wore an 'iron belt' as a token of penance and was an assiduous pilgrim to distant Scottish shrines like that of St Ninian at Whithorn and that of St Dutho at Tain. These pilgrimages were no austere affairs to mortify the flesh. He would set out for Tain accompanied by a poet, three falconers, a horse laden with silver plate, four Italian minstrels and a Moorish drummer (and a payment to 'five loud minstrels' suggests that the King liked a lot of noise); and it was quite in character that *en route* to the shrine he would pay a visit to his mistress at Darnaway. But, not content with Scottish pilgrimages, King James also contemplated a pilgrimage to the Holy Land. This project merged easily in the grander one of a crusade. Keenly interested in the development of a Scottish navy, for which he built the great *Michael*, which was far the largest ship of her time, he saw himself as the admiral of an expedition by united Christendom against the Turks.

For this project James has been much censured, as 'infatuated' and as 'a moonstruck romantic'. And it is true that, superficially viewed, his project looks back to the ideas of his ancestors Robert I and James I, whose hearts were carried into battle against the infidel. But the fact is that by this time the Turks were threatening central Europe and a dozen years after James's death they were at the gates of Vienna. An alliance of the princes of Europe against the invaders would have made very good sense. Nor was talk of a crusade the monopoly of James, for it was something of a fashion at the time. But to contemporary sovereigns like Henry VII, Ferdinand of Aragon, Louis XII of France and the Emperor Maximilian—a pack of 'hoary intriguers' as they have been called—the concept was merely a hollow pretence or a diplomatic fiction. They lacked James's breadth of vision, and their only interest was their own aggrandisement. To make matters worse, another of those hard and selfish princes was the pope himself, to whom James looked in vain for leadership of the crusade.

This pope, Julius II, was concerned to maintain and extend the states of the Church in central Italy and to compete with the growing national monarchies in the secular sphere. He tried by adroit combinations to deal with his enemies in detail. Thus, in the League of Cambrai (1508), he used the French to overcome Venice, and then he made an alliance with Venice in order to expel the French from Italy. By 1511 he had induced Ferdinand of Aragon, Venice and Henry VIII to range themselves against Louis XII in the so-called Holy League, which the Emperor joined later. 'A passionate, warlike spirit, better fitted for violent activity than for meditation.... This pope, endowed with the gifts of a warrior, did not hesitate to lead in person more than one expedition, to the stupefaction of a Europe which was nevertheless accustomed to spectacles which would appear scandalous today.... The most spectacular episode of these wars was the siege and capture of the fortress of Mirandola in midwinter; the pope, helmeted, directed the operations in person. ... His prowess earned the admiration of some, but it scandalised enlightened people, and rightly so.'* Such a pope might flatter King James's ambitions by sending him a hat and a sword which he had blessed—the sword is still to be seen in Edinburgh Castle—but he was not likely to commission him to lead a crusade.

Pope Julius, primarily a politician, had indeed formed a Holy League, which was what James had been agitating for, but that League was directed not against the infidel but against the Most Christian King of France, the ancient ally of the Scots. Louis XII then made a tactical, but understandable, error by appealing to a general council against the pope and this gave Julius an excuse for denouncing Louis as schismatic. The critical fact for Scotland was that Henry VIII of England was now a member of the alliance aimed at France, and James found himself in an awkward situation. Already, before the formation of the League, he had been alarmed at the breach between the pope and France, and his fresh efforts for peace and a crusade included the circulation of an appeal to the princes of Europe. Only after the Holy League had been concluded and Henry VIII drawn into it, and only under

**New Cambridge Modern History*, i, 81

persuasion from Louis, who was lavish with promises of what he would do to further James's crusade, did the Scottish King consent to renew the Scottish alliance with France (in 1512), and at the same time he wrote to the pope reproaching him bitterly for dividing instead of uniting Christendom. Confronted by a pope allied with England and ready to abuse his spiritual powers for political ends, James was at a double disadvantage: not only did he find himself the ally of a King of France who had been declared schismatic, but his own undertakings to England were fortified by ecclesiastical sanctions, owing to the papal confirmation of the treaty of perpetual peace of 1502.

The relations between Scotland and England were soon disturbed by incidents at sea and on the Borders, and were not improved by the pretensions to superior virtue of Englishmen who conceived themselves to be fighting the battle of Holy Church. Scottish goods were seized by 'Englishmen calling themselves the pope's men', Scottish ships were plundered on the pretext of 'service to Julius II'; and the English ambassador told James that all the world knew that King Henry was acting against France in the cause of the Church—to which James retorted that Henry was fortunate to have such an obliging pope. It all amounted to this, that although the Holy League was purely political, Julius thought that he could use his spiritual powers as supreme pontiff to further his political aims and to keep the Scots neutral while England attacked France. It has been said that the behaviour of Julius at this juncture was like that of a referee in a football match who dons a jersey and plays for one of the sides, but retains his whistle and insists on declaring his opponents offside whenever they become at all dangerous.*

When an English army actually invaded France in 1513, even although it was in the name of the pope's precious Holy League, James could not stand aside, although he risked ecclesiastical censures. When he died at Flodden (9 September), he was under sentence of excommunication, and papal prestige in Scotland

*J. D. Mackie, in *Trans. Roy. Hist. Soc.*, 4th series, xxix, 109

probably never recovered from the abuse to which papal power had been put by Julius II.

James's purpose in leading his army across the frontier was not to penetrate deeply into England, but to draw English forces to the north, and from this point of view his generalship was sound. He systematically reduced three castles on the English side of the frontier, and accusations that he wasted his time are groundless. Nor were his tactics immediately before the battle indefensible. But once the forces were engaged there was no longer any unity in the Scottish command, if indeed any command at all. It had been remarked when James was a much younger man that he was not a good captain, because he started to fight before he had given his orders, and he had not learned much more wisdom since then. Possibly the greatest weakness of the Scots in the first phase of the engagement was the mismanagement of their artillery. The guns were there on which James had expended much time and money and which impressed the victors after the battle as 'marvellous large pieces of ordnance', but the skilled gunners had been sent away with the fleet to France and it was amateurs who were in the field to mishandle the Scottish artillery. The English guns, on the other hand, were well directed, and it was the execution which they started to do on the Scottish ranks that compelled James to move down Branxton Hill with his division and start the engagement. Refusing advice to stay where he could retain command, he rushed on with his men, leaving the leaders of the other divisions to act without any concerted plan.

The Scots fought on foot, and their principal weapon was a long spear. Arranged in phalanx formation, bodies of men armed with such weapons were almost irresistible as long as they kept their ranks and were on the move: with sufficient momentum, they were likely to drive everything before them and were not likely to be overcome save by artillery from a distance. But if the phalanx was broken up, or if it was brought to a standstill, the situation was quite different. The spear was a cumbersome, almost a useless, weapon, for a stationary man to try to use at close quarters. The English, on their side, were armed with the bill, a weapon with a sturdy shaft surmounted with a broad blade—a weapon which, in strong hands, could inflict a fearful wound and which, moreover, was admirably suited for cutting through the shafts of spears. Once the Scots came to a standstill, at the foot of Branxton Hill, the English were able to hack at their spear-shafts with the bills and render them useless. The Scots, deprived of their spears, had to resort to their swords, but the sword in turn was useless against the longer bill. The result was a massacre, at least for some of the Scottish divisions.

The English claimed that the number of Scots killed was no fewer than 10,000. This would have amounted to about half of the full strength of James's army, and is likely to be an over-estimate. But if the total number of deaths is uncertain, there is no doubt about the losses of notables: one of the casualties was Alexander Stewart, the young Archbishop of St Andrews (though, if he was as short-sighted as Erasmus says, he can have been of little use in battle), and with him fell two bishops, two abbots and two dozen earls and lords. At the head of the death-roll was the name of the King himself. He is said to have killed five men with his spear before it was shattered, and when he fell he was pierced by an arrow and gashed by a bill. 'O what a noble and triumphaunt courage was thys for a Kyng to fyghte in a battayll as a meane souldier.'*

**Hall's Chronicle* (London, 1809), 562

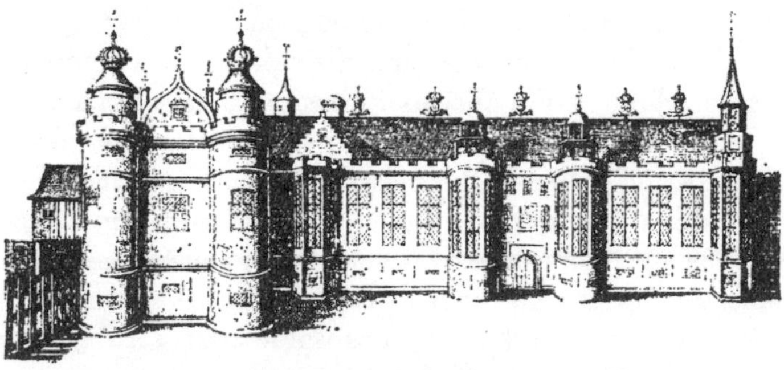

34 Holyrood Palace, showing the James IV tower
From an engraving by De Wit after Gordon of Rothiemay, 1647

8

James the Ill-Beloved: James V, 1513-42

The accession of James V initiated yet another minority, and an uncommonly long one, for the new King had been born on 10 April 1512 and was therefore little more than a year old when his father was killed. Not only was it a long minority, but a minority in which the course of events was exceedingly complex and tortuous, more tortuous even than those troubled years of Crichton and Livingston under James II and of Kennedy and Boyd under James III. On the other hand, while the complexity of the situation is such as almost to repel a reader, there are other features which make it deserving of study. For one thing, there is now much more ample information available, including a vast amount of correspondence in which contemporaries committed their thoughts to paper. We can no longer complain that we are wholly at a loss to understand the motives of the persons involved in Scottish affairs; they have become figures of flesh and blood and we can form some impression of their aims and purposes. More than that, it becomes important, increasingly throughout the reign, that motives are no longer merely personal, but are based on some principle, either political or religious.

For two centuries, while there had been faction in plenty, it had been mainly selfish in origin, and questions of politics, far less of statesmanship, had been little in evidence. But in the two generations after Flodden Scotland was divided on a political question—the question of the relations of Scotland with England and France—and this question was soon bound up with a religious question—the attitude of Scotland to the Reformation. There is no period of Scottish history in which Scottish affairs were so largely shaped by developments in other countries rather than by events at home. Consequently, the historian must constantly keep in view not only the international situation but even the situation inside England and inside France, and the explanation of what was happening in Scotland is very often to be found beyond Scotland's own frontiers.

The reign began with what looks very like a familiar situation. Twice before, in the minorities of James II and James III, we have encountered a Queen Mother who is, naturally, the guardian of her young son, the King, and who complicates matters by seeking consolation with a subject for the loss of her husband—Joan Beaufort, the widow of James I, who married Stewart of Lorne, and Mary of Gueldres, the widow of James II, who associated with Hepburn of Hailes. This time a similar part was played by Margaret Tudor. But Margaret Tudor differed from those earlier Queens in two ways, for she was the sister of the reigning King of England and she was conspicuously unstable in her affections. Indeed, her matrimonial adventures came near to rivalling those of her brother, Henry VIII. She was married first to James IV, then to the Earl of Angus (whose name she appropriately spelled as 'Anguisshe'); she divorced Angus in order to marry Lord Methven (who appears in her letters as 'Muffin'), and from Methven in turn she sought a divorce with a view to being reunited with the discarded Angus; she was also suspected more than once of aiming at a match with the Duke of Albany. This was the woman who, in terms of James IV's will, was tutrix to her son as long as she remained a widow, and therefore head of the government.

After Flodden there was no panic in Scotland, and little hesitation or discord. The Scottish losses in the battle, partly because they included that of the King, have captured the romantic imagination of later generations, and the popular impression of the defeat has been expressed in, and shaped by, spirited verses. Sir Walter Scott, in *Marmion*, related that

Though bill-men ply the ghastly blow,
Unbroken was the ring;
The stubborn spear-men still made good
Their dark impenetrable wood,
Each stepping where his comrade stood
The instant that he fell.

William Edmonstoune Aytoun, in *Edinburgh after Flodden*, imagines a solitary, wounded soldier returning to Edinburgh to report:

No one failed him. He is keeping
Royal state and semblance still;
Knight and noble lie around him,
Cold on Flodden's fatal hill.

And the song to the effect that 'The Flowers o' the Forest are a' wede awa'' concentrated on the supposed heavy losses among the Borderers—who, according to reliable evidence, seem rather to have taken good care to preserve themselves. The contemporary attitude to the battle gives no support to the romantic imaginings. There was, after all, nothing novel about a heavy defeat at the hands of the English, and Flodden was neither the first nor the last in a long series—Falkirk, Halidon, Homildon, Solway Moss, Pinkie, Preston, Dunbar, Worcester. It would have been surprising if Flodden had been thought of either as an irretrievable disaster or as a reason for changing Scottish policy. The Scots had no thought of capitulating to England or of abandoning the alliance with France. Flodden had been fought in September, and it was too late to conduct a further campaign in 1513, but the Scots were thinking in terms of a renewal of the war in the following spring and made preparations to that end.

It may well have seemed difficult to reconcile such a policy with acceptance of Margaret Tudor as head of the government, and it is not surprising that the alternative was soon considered that a Governor for Scotland should be supplied from France, in the person of John, Duke of Albany. He was the son of James III's troublesome brother, Alexander, who had died in France in 1484 after marrying a French lady. Duke John, born in 1481, was now heir to the Scottish crown after the young James V and his younger brother, who was born posthumously and died in 1515. As heir presumptive, Albany could very reasonably go to Scotland and claim the office of Governor. Next in the line of succession after Albany (who was childless) stood James Hamilton, Earl of Arran, the son of James II's daughter Mary. Arran, as the native-born Scot nearest the throne, might have challenged Albany's claim, but it is clear that, if he was not actually one of those who initially proposed Albany's candidature for the governorship, he supported it.

In November 1513 a general council agreed to the suggestion that Albany should come to Scotland with men and munitions, and acceded to the request of the French King that the league should be renewed. Albany, however, did not come, for King Louis did not share the Scottish confidence that the war would be renewed when weather for campaigning returned, and was instead moving towards a truce with England, which was actually made in the spring. An uneasy and uncertain situation continued until the autumn of 1514, when two events occurred which changed decisively the prospects of Scotland and its young King. Queen Margaret, a widow of twenty-four, married Archibald Douglas, sixth Earl of Angus, who was slightly her junior. Angus was the grandson of old 'Bell-the-Cat', who had led the opposition to James III in 1482, and therefore a member of a family which had a record of instability and disaffection; and he was described by his uncle as a young witless fool. But a marriage to any subject automatically lowered the Queen's status, and it also terminated her legal rights as tutrix to her son. In the same month as Margaret married Angus, Henry of England and Louis XII of France made a treaty whereby Louis married Henry's younger

THE SUCCESSION IN THE SIXTEENTH CENTURY

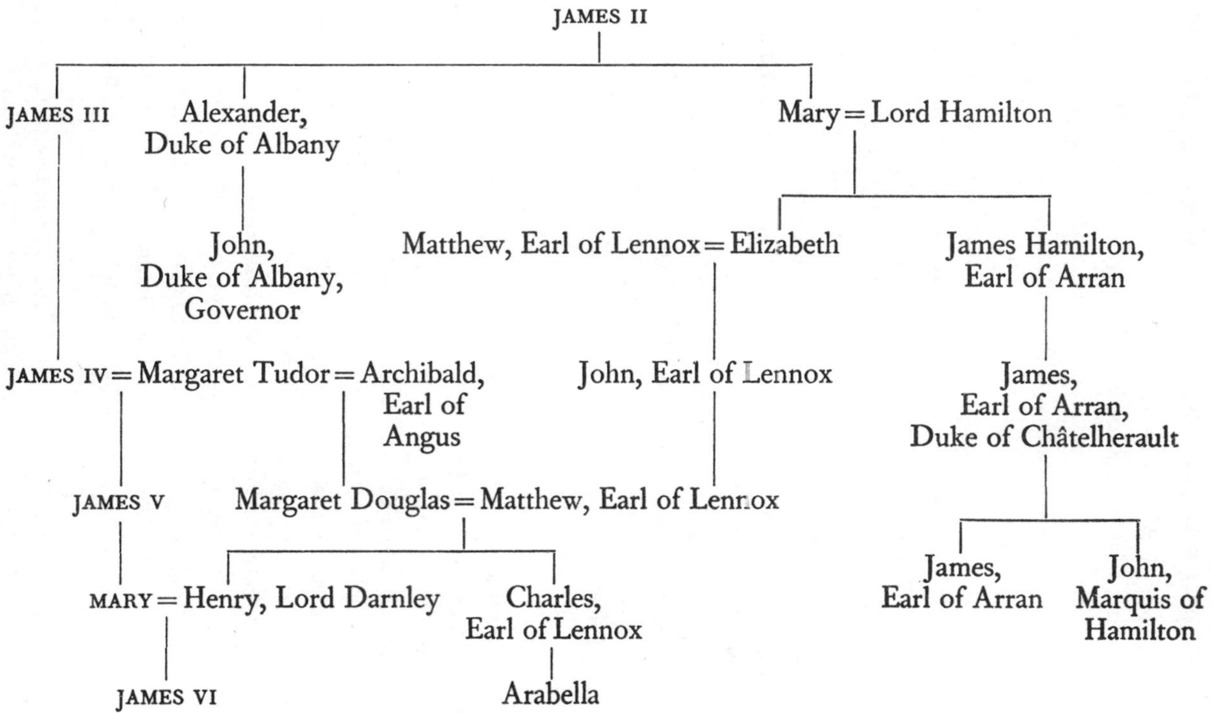

sister, Mary. The first of these two events cleared the way for the acceptance of Albany as Governor of Scotland, but the second meant that France no longer had any need of Scotland as an ally.

The Scottish estates, after formally declaring that Margaret had lost her rights, renewed the invitation to Albany to 'come home' with all possible haste. But, whereas what the Scots still had in mind was a renewal of war, Albany was released by France and sent to Scotland in 1515 not with men and munitions to resume war but with advice to the Scots to keep the peace.

Albany was received with enthusiasm, but soon encountered opposition. It may have arisen partly out of disappointment with his foreign policy, but it was based mainly on personal jealousies and on distrust between the Governor and some of the Scottish nobles. Margaret was compelled by a show of force to give up her children and, with Angus, was easily driven out of the country. More serious trouble was made for Albany by a faction led by Lord Home. His family, like that of Angus, had a bad record, for his father had headed the rebellion which cost James III his life, and he himself had played such a dubious part at Flodden that he was even suspected of having murdered James IV after the battle. Propaganda among disgruntled Scots could make much of the fact that only the lives of two young boys stood between Albany and the throne, and the growth of suspicion may have been all the easier because Albany could speak only French. He was, besides, an expensive visitor, whose household cost more than a poor country could well afford, and the Frenchmen who came in his train were unpopular.

Yet Albany's record as active Governor was by no means a discreditable one. He seems to have been unquestionably loyal to the young King, and declined to send either of the royal boys to France—whereas some of his enemies plotted to hand them over to Henry VIII. He supported whole-heartedly the Scottish defiance of the pope after allegiance to Rome had been strained by Julius II's attitude before Flodden. He took steps to strengthen the administration of justice and to punish law-breakers. Yet—although we are told that when he was opposed or contradicted he would in a fit of anger throw his bonnet into the fire—he was not vindictive and instead pursued an intelligent policy of appeasement. Of the rebel lords, Home alone was executed; with others the Governor was soon reconciled; Margaret was offered the chance of returning to Scotland if she would undertake to be 'ane gud Scottis woman'; and Angus was pardoned. It may well have contributed to the general acquiescence in Albany's rule that, so far as can be seen, he came round to the Scottish point of view on foreign policy and endeavoured to stimulate France into renewing her undertakings to support the Scots against England.

It was evidently with the intention of influencing the French attitude to Scotland that Albany went back to France in 1517. He was successful to the extent of bringing about the conclusion of the Treaty of Rouen, which provided that France and Scotland should act jointly and give mutual assistance in the event of an English attack on either of them. France also held out to the young Scottish King certain hypothetical prospects of a French bride. King Francis had at this time two daughters, but the elder, Louise, was pledged to the King of Spain, and the younger, Charlotte, was to be substituted for Louise should she die. All that was available for King James was the reversion of Charlotte should she not be required elsewhere, or, failing her, another daughter of the French King should one be born. Actually, one of the existing daughters died very soon, leaving no one available for James. Yet the prospects opened by this treaty had a strong influence on the calculations of successive Scottish governments and of James himself as he grew to maturity, and it was largely owing to his personal persistence that in the end, twenty years later, he did marry a daughter of the French King.

At the time, however, the Treaty of Rouen was no more than a paper success for Albany's diplomacy. The Governor found that by going to France he had lost his freedom of action and that his movements were once more to be controlled in the interests of France. He had undertaken to return to Scotland in four months, but he was detained in France for four years. Francis was still the ally of Henry VIII, who insisted successfully that Albany should not be allowed to return to Scotland, and it was not French policy to do anything to stimulate Scottish action against England. The situation also dictated that the Treaty of Rouen should remain unratified.

During Albany's absence it became apparent that, while a Governor of his birth and personal influence could do something to control faction while he was in the country, the rivalries and feuds of the nobles tended as ever to produce confusion during a minority. It seems that Albany had designated a Frenchman, De la Bastie, to preside in his absence over a council of regency consisting of four earls—Angus, Arran, Huntly and Argyll. But De la Bastie was murdered as a result of a feud with the Home family (whose head had been executed by Albany), and that 'young witless fool', Angus, soon wearied of co-operating with the other earls in the tasks of government. Not only did Angus become an obstacle to good government and a focus for disaffected and troublesome elements, but he had a hold on the capital which gravely embarrassed the administration. This was the background to the picturesque affray in the streets of Edinburgh in 1520 known as 'Cleanse the Causeway,' when Arran's followers, the Hamiltons, miscalculated their strength and were driven out of the town by the Angus Douglases. It was for excellent reasons that at this point the town council ordained that the provost should have a guard of four halberdiers 'becaus the warld is brukle and trublous'; they still accompany the Lord Provost on formal occasions and so recall the turbulent minority of James V.

There could be no relief for the distracted country until the international situation permitted the return of Albany. In 1521 Henry VIII came to an agreement with the Emperor Charles V to join in an attack on France. King Francis was thus free from his undertakings to Henry and ready to revert to the traditional French policy of using Scotland to provide a distraction for English forces. Consequently, in November 1521 Albany came back to Scotland. This time he came as the advocate of Franco-Scottish co-operation against England, and to encourage the Scots

Francis now ratified the Treaty of Rouen. The marriage provision it contained had become a shade more realistic, for the Princess Madeleine, born in 1520, was available as a bride for King James. Albany found, however, that such encouragement was not enough, for his military preparations met with opposition: the Scots were not going to invade England on the instructions of France. Albany thought they might be more co-operative if he could demonstrate that French backing was a reality, so he went over to France in 1522 and returned in 1523, bringing with him a very considerable military force, as well as money and supplies. But the Scots were not impressed. Albany did muster a large army, but it showed from the outset that it was ill-disciplined and when it reached the Tweed there was an almost superstitious dread of crossing the frontier. The Scots, it is clear, had now had time to reflect on the significance of Flodden, which they saw as a disaster which had arisen from a campaign undertaken in a war which Scotland herself had not sought but which had been the consequence of the French alliance; and some of them were coming round to the view that there might be more future in collaboration with England than in antagonism.

Albany, frustrated in his furtherance of the French policy, left Scotland once more in May 1524, and the existence of two rival political parties was at once demonstrated. The Earl of Arran, whose claim to authority through his position as the native-born Scot nearest to the throne had been greatly strengthened by Albany's departure and by the death of the Duchess of Albany without surviving children, came to terms with Queen Margaret and, with the support of other nobles, 'erected' the twelve-year-old King; that is, they invested him in person with the symbols of sovereignty, so formally bringing Albany's governorship to an end. The foreign policy of the new administration was made clear in a letter sent by King James on 5 August to his 'derrest and richt inteirlye weil beluffit uncle, the King of Inglande', intimating that he had put an end to the authority of Albany (who had been something of a *bête noire* to Henry). When the estates met in November, Albany was declared to have lost his offices of tutor and Governor. But the decision was not unanimous. While Arran argued on behalf of the material advantages of a treaty with England, Archbishop James Beaton of St Andrews urged that the Scots should remain loyal to Albany and maintain the league with France, and he received considerable support.

The *coup d'état* did not produce a stable administration, largely because of the personal relationship between Margaret and Angus, from whom she had long sought a divorce. Angus was appointed one of the Queen's advisers, but there was no possibility of holding the capricious Margaret in any combination which included her husband. Therefore, as Angus had become the premier agent of the English interest in Scotland—it was remarked that he would serve Henry better than five Earls of Arran—Margaret now moved towards an accommodation with France. Angus steadily increased his influence, and ultimately established his ascendancy by a *coup* which gave him sole control of the King whose name was essential to any administration. It had been arranged that James should remain in the hands of each of the four principal magnates in turn, but when the time came for Angus to give up the King he kept the boy in his own hands.

Thus we enter on the final phase of this minority. Just as Livingstons had finally emerged as the leading family in the minority of James II, and Boyds in that of James III, so the ultimate beneficiaries in the minority of James V were Angus and the Douglases. On 14 June 1526 there was a kind of fresh 'erection' of the King, now fourteen years old: it was declared that authority was in his hands, and this was a device to deprive any competitor of Angus, the King's keeper, of pretensions to power. In 1527 Angus became chancellor. He appointed his uncle as treasurer, his brother as master of the household, James Douglas of Drumlanrig as master of the wine-cellar and James Douglas of Parkhead as master of the larder, so that, with Douglases dominating the household as well as the administration, the King was constantly under surveillance and was in effect a prisoner. As Angus progressively appropriated offices to his kinsmen, he alienated the other magnates, but it was impossible to overthrow him as long as the King was in his hands; and George Douglas, Angus's brother, declared that should the King's body be torn apart in an attempt at rescue the Douglases would still keep a part of it. Two attempts at rescue were made, but both failed.

In 1528, however, the King managed to open a channel of communication with his mother, who was able to put Stirling Castle at his disposal. Escaping from Edinburgh, he made his way to Stirling, where he was soon surrounded by a large and influential body of magnates who were only too ready to rally against Angus. The Douglases were declared to have detained the King's person for two years against his will, they were forfeited and they fled to England, where they remained for the rest of the reign.

At this point we come to the end of this long and troubled minority. But much had happened which was to shape the course of events for the remaining years of James V's life. The King's bitterness against Angus and his family was unrelenting. At the outset, Angus had been in the unpromising position of a stepfather; he had been not only a stepfather, but a stepfather with whom the King's mother was soon at loggerheads and against whom she did her best to influence her son. To make matters worse, Angus had been James's gaoler for a couple of years. Out of those personal relationships there emerged facts which were to be of great political importance. Angus and his faction, from whom James was thus alienated, had been the pro-English faction, or at least its more militant wing. In reaction against Angus, therefore, James was almost inevitably driven to an anti-English and pro-French policy, and this had far-reaching consequences for later history. Andrew Lang drew attention to the significance of it all: 'James became implacable to the whole Douglas name. . . . But to shake off and break down the Douglases, a thing desirable in itself, was to turn away from England, the patron of the Douglases, to turn away from Protestantism, to court France, and to choose the doomed cause of Catholicism in the north. These dull and squalid intrigues of a selfish, sensual termagant [Margaret], and her unscrupulously ambitious husband Angus, determined the fate of the Stuart line. They were to lean on France, and were to lose three crowns for a mass. Exile, the executioner's axe, and broken hearts were to be their reward in a secular series of sorrows flowing from the long minority and unhappy environment of James V.'* Lang, as usual, exaggerates, but there is some truth in what he says.

There were, of course, more profound reasons than antipathy to Angus which impelled James V to favour France rather than England. Whether any impression had been made on his mind by Albany himself, who left Scotland for the last time when James was only twelve, may be doubted, but the memory of the Albany régime may well have contrasted favourably in his recollections with that of Angus. Another influence on the King's childhood was that of Gavin Dunbar, who was his 'master' or tutor from the beginning of 1517 until 1525. Dunbar had presumably been appointed tutor by Albany, and in 1524 he became Archbishop of Glasgow on Albany's recommendation, so it may be inferred that he favoured the pro-French policy. He was reported in 1525 to be 'wholly given in favour of the Duke of Albany'. When James escaped from Angus he at once made Dunbar his chancellor. It hardly seems that the King allowed the chancellor to direct policy, or even to guide his own direction of it, but the sentiments and thought which James brought to the work of government clearly owed much to the influence of this supporter of the French alliance. In any event, Albany's own influence in Scotland did not expire with his departure from the country, for he continued to act as a Scottish agent in international diplomacy and he had a material link with Scotland to the extent that Dunbar Castle continued to be garrisoned in his name. James, besides, was well aware that, in terms of a treaty drawn up in his childhood, there was in France a princess designated as his bride.

Matrimony may not, indeed, have been much in the King's mind except for reasons of state. His intellectual education does not seem to have been as neglected as has sometimes been sup-

*Andrew Lang, *History of Scotland*, i, 409

posed, either in those very early days when he had been cared for by Sir David Lindsay, the poet, who remarked to the King

The first syllabis thou didst mute
Was Pa Da Lin *upon thy lute,*

or throughout the years when the royal tutor was Gavin Dunbar, a 'wise councillor and chancellor' who had much to do with the final organisation of Scotland's central court for civil justice. But the whole background of James's upbringing was conducive to moral delinquency, and it was said that Angus not only neglected to provide the King with suitable companions but encouraged him in a precocious career of vice. When he was still under twenty he already had three illegitimate sons, and the total recorded number was seven, all by different mothers. It may be to his credit that he did occasionally contemplate marriage to one of his mistresses, which would at least have secured the succession.

There were, however, compelling reasons for marriage, and for marriage to a foreign princess, because only by a large dowry was James's most pressing need likely to be satisfied. His policy as a ruler, and the whole course of events during his active reign, were as a matter of fact very largely determined by the financial situation which he inherited from the governments of the minority. That the finances of the royal household had never recovered from the strain imposed by the costly visits of Albany is suggested by the fact that in 1527 a baker was suing for £82 16*s*. in respect of bread which had been delivered to the Governor in 1516. Margaret and Angus did not feel that they had any duty to husband the resources of the crown, and by the late 1520s the financial officers were lamenting that they were managing to operate only by the expenditure of their 'awin geir' and intimating that they could 'sustene na forrer'.

In short, there was bankruptcy, and only if fresh sources of revenue could be tapped would it be possible to maintain the government as the King grew to manhood. It might, indeed, be practicable to continue the policy of earlier kings and enrich the crown through the forfeiture of peccant nobles, but it was unpredictable how far reasons or pretexts might be found for such action. Much more promising prospects could be detected along two other lines—the wealth of the Church and the dowry which could be expected on the King's marriage. Proceedings in relation to the nobles were a matter for domestic policy, except in so far as treasonable dealings with England might lead to forfeiture; but relations with the Church in Scotland involved negotiations with the pope and were connected with the question of the Scottish attitude to the Reformation, which was an international movement, and the question of the dowry which would come with a foreign princess was a matter of Scotland's place in the international setting. Thus the financial needs of James V raised the whole issue of foreign, as well as domestic, policy.

Conditions were peculiarly favourable to Scotland. Both ecclesiastical and foreign affairs were dominated by the progress of the Reformation. Luther's revolt had started in 1517, and Lutheran ideas very soon made a marked impression on Scotland by way of the east coast ports, which were in constant communication with the Continent. As early as 1525 the Scottish parliament passed an act against the importation of Lutheran books. The Scottish government began to realise, even before James V emerged from tutelage, that its attitude to the Reformation could be used as a lever to obtain concessions from the pope, for in 1527 a letter went to Rome announcing that the King of Scots would not suffer Lutheranism to invade his dominions and would thus hope to earn an extension of the ancient privileges of his crown. A little later, James followed up one letter to the pope in which he expressed his resolve 'to banish the foul Lutheran sect' with another in which he demanded that the pope should ratify the privileges of Scottish kings. In short, the Scottish crown promised orthodoxy—at a price. Neither the pope nor the Scottish churchmen found it easy, or even possible, to resist this argument.

The European political situation, too, gave James V a great opportunity. At this stage the Scottish historian has to think not only of a triangle of England, Scotland and France, but of a quadrilateral, for the Empire was concerned as well. The Emperor Charles V was always guided mainly by the persistent rivalry between his House of Hapsburg and the French House of Valois, and while he was sometimes at peace with Francis I there was never any reality or security behind the treaties into which they entered. But, at the time when James V began to direct Scottish policy, Charles was alienated not only from Francis but also from Henry VIII of England, who in 1527 had started those proceedings which led in the end to his divorce from Catharine of Aragon, the Emperor's aunt. Charles calculated that, should he ever launch a campaign against England, it would be useful to have Scotland as an ally, and he was not unwilling to see her detached from her traditional association with France. France, mainly because of the threat to her from the Emperor, was at this time allied with England and anxious to ensure at least England's neutrality. Therefore, as was usual in such phases, she had no interest in an effective alliance with Scotland and was not going to risk offending England by fulfilling the Treaty of Rouen and providing a bride for the Scottish King.

James had probably no real interest in an imperial alliance, but he saw an opportunity to threaten France with his defection from her side to that of the Emperor and thereby stimulate Francis into the fulfilment of his engagements to Scotland. Already before the end of 1527 it had been suggested that James might marry the Emperor's sister Mary, widow of the King of Hungary, and in 1529 an envoy was sent from Scotland to inspect the lady. Whatever James may have thought, Mary made it plain that she regarded a marriage to him with abhorrence. However, other imperial brides were possible: Christian II, the deposed King of Denmark, had married a sister of the Emperor, and in 1528 he offered the Scottish King one of his daughters, with a view to obtaining Scottish help towards the recovery of his throne. Talk of a marriage between James and one of 'the Emperor's nieces of Denmark' went on intermittently for six or seven years.

Into the course of the negotiations with the Emperor there

intruded for a time another proposal, which originated with the Duke of Albany. Albany was far too strongly committed to the interests of France to regard an imperial marriage with any favour, but he was enough of a realist to know that a French marriage was impossible as long as the Anglo-French amity lasted. Therefore in 1527 and again in 1530 he proposed the marriage of James to his own niece, Catharine de' Medici, who was the ward of Pope Clement VII. This plan did not appeal to Francis, who, though positive that he would not concede his own daughter to James, was unwilling to let him marry elsewhere, and he effectively torpedoed the scheme by arranging the marriage of Catharine to his own son, afterwards Henry II. Nor did the proposal appeal much to the pope, who could not face the prospect of letting his niece depart for what he regarded as a remote and cold country.

The outcome of the proposed match with Catharine was curious and unexpected. It can most easily be explained on the assumption that the Scots had been very candid in admitting that they were less interested in Catharine than in her dowry and that the pope in effect said that he was not going to part with his niece but would arrange ample financial compensation for King James. The compensation came not out of the pope's pocket but out of the pockets of the Scottish clergy. At any rate, in July 1531, four months after Catharine's hand had been refused to James, the pope authorised the Scottish King to collect a perpetual tax of £10,000 a year from the Scottish prelacies and a levy of one-tenth of all Scottish ecclesiastical revenues for the limited period of three years. Generosity on such a startling scale cannot be accounted for wholly by the negotiations about Catharine, and the papal attitude is partly explained by a sense of urgency and crisis arising out of events in England. Henry VIII had recently been acknowledged as Head of the Church of England, and the pope was anxious to ensure that Scotland would not go the same way.

The levy of the three tenths was on the ground of the need to strengthen and protect the Scottish state; the pretext for the permanent tax of £10,000 a year was the establishment of a College of Justice. The development of an effective central court for civil cases, which had gone a long way under James IV, had been temporarily arrested after Flodden but had been resumed in the 1520s, and by 1528 there was in practice a Court of Session, consisting largely of at least semi-professional lawyers and holding regular sittings. Because of the finance now provided by papal action, James V is apt to be remembered as 'the founder of the Court of Session', but all that really happened was the endowment of a court which already existed. Of the fifteen judges nominated to the 'College of Justice' in 1532, all but one had been active in the Court of Session in the previous year, and eleven had been active as far back as 1527. The fact that the 'lords of session' now became 'senators of the College of Justice' was a formal change in nomenclature which would sound impressive in the ears of the Italians who arranged for the pope to authorise finance.

In May 1532 the Scottish parliament passed legislation designed to demonstrate that the King's orthodoxy had been secured—for a consideration—and to show the pope that he proposed to earn his money. Its first act recited a declaration by the King remarking—with truth—that while earlier popes had been gracious to Scottish Kings, 'Pape Clement, now pape of Rome, hes bene mair gracius and benevolent till his grace than to all his forbearis,' and recorded the King's resolution to defend the authority of 'the sete of Rome and halikirk'. The second act related the King's intention to 'institute ane college of cunning and wise men . . . for the administration of justice in civil actions'. In fact, while judicial salaries were necessary, no one can ever have believed that the King had any intention of spending £10,000 a year, or anything like it, on a College of Justice, while the Scottish clergy, for their part, had no desire to shoulder a permanent tax. What happened in the end was that the prelates compounded for £72,000, to be paid in four years to the crown for no specified purpose, and assigned the beggarly sum of £1,400 a year in perpetuity for the salaries of the judges.

There were elements in the situation which made it not unreasonable that churchmen should contribute to the endowment of a central civil court. For one thing, the president and seven of the fourteen judges were to be ecclesiastics, and the development of the court had owed a good deal to Archbishop Dunbar. Secondly, as the emergence of Protestant thought resulted in a contempt for the judgments of the ecclesiastical courts, and laymen could no longer be browbeaten into paying their dues to the Church by the threat of excommunication, it was to the interest of the clergy to be able to resort to an effective secular court. But there was yet another factor. In 1532 the pope conceded that no Scottish case was to be called to Rome in the first instance, but was to be judged in Scotland by ecclesiastics appointed by the King, provided that he remained obedient to Rome. This is surely to be read in the light of Henry VIII's prohibition of appeals to Rome: in this matter as in others, James of Scotland was gaining much of the substance which Henry gained, but without any formal breach with the papacy.

The three tenths and the 'Great Tax' had been an unexpected windfall, almost a by-product of diplomacy which was concerned mainly with the question of a bride for the King. It remained to be seen whether that primary objective, also, would be attained. James continued to exploit his favourable opportunities with singular skill, and for a few years Scotland and its King played a part in the international scene in almost ludicrous disproportion to the real importance of the country. The continued negotiations with the Emperor, which brought James the order of the Golden Fleece, raised his price in the English and French markets, with the consequence that he received the orders of the Garter and St Michael as well. The four-sided negotiations which went on until 1536 were tortuous and, in so far as they were inconclusive, they form no part of the history of Scotland, which was affected only by the upshot. The reply of France to Scottish representations was for a long time almost stereotyped: the Princess Madeleine, who was available for James in terms of the Treaty of Rouen, was too young, or too frail, for marriage—

which was to prove true enough. But at a later stage, after James's persistent negotiations with the Emperor stimulated France to make a counterbid, and after the French began to care less for the susceptibilities of Henry VIII, Francis was moved to offer another French lady in place of the delicate Madeleine. By the end of 1534 he offered the daughter of the Duke of Vendôme, with a dowry of 100,000 crowns; James, after seeing the lady's portrait, stipulated for a good deal more. A settlement along these lines was agreed on at the beginning of 1536.

But even then James seems to have kept the powers guessing as to his final intentions, and not until he was actually on his way to France as a prospective bridegroom was a French marriage a certainty. Even then, the marriage which took place was not to Marie de Vendôme, whom James found to be *bossue et contrefaite* (hunch-backed and misshapen) and even more disappointing than her portrait had suggested. The marriage was to the oft-refused Madeleine, whose own insistence seems to have overcome her father's doubts, and the ceremony took place in Paris on 1 January 1537. Death next intervened, for the wretched Madeleine survived her arrival in Scotland for only seven weeks. There seems to have been no hesitation, and little delay, in finding a second French bride. The choice was Mary of Guise-Lorraine, whom James had met in Paris when he was there in the winter of 1536–7 and who had been widowed by the death of her first husband, the Duc de Longueville, a month before James lost his first wife.

The marriages—and the dowries which accompanied them—implied a bargain, and Scotland's part was to commit herself to a firm alliance with France and with the Roman Church. A few days after the marriage to Madeleine the pope sent James a sword and a cap with an intimation that he hoped for Scottish co-operation, along with France, in a campaign against the schismatic Henry VIII. The principal agent in arranging the marriage with Mary of Guise was David Beaton, nephew and coadjutor to the Archbishop of St Andrews and leader of pro-French and orthodox opinion in Scotland. Scotland was thus tied to France and the papacy.

But James was to find that he could not carry his people with him in the foreign policy he had chosen. One reason was the ever-increasing tendency to question the wisdom of continued hostility to England, another was the growth in Scotland of opinions favourable to ecclesiastical reform and therefore opposed to a campaign against an England which had rejected the papacy. But it was also true that many features of James's domestic policy were alienating his subjects and destroying their confidence in him.

James shared the determination of his predecessors to extend royal power in the Borders and in the Highlands, but his measures were marked by unusual ruthlessness and by a disregard of the tactical wisdom of conciliating certain elements while repressing others. Almost at the outset, in his dealings with the Borderers, he showed his merciless nature in his treatment of 'Johnnie Armstrong', who remarked (so at least a ballad relates) as he was led to execution:

I have asked grace at a graceless face:
There is nane for my men and me.

Practically all the Border lairds were in prison at one time or another—Lord Maxwell, the Earl of Bothwell (who was finally banished), Scott of Branxholm (who was imprisoned for the King's lifetime), Ker of Ferniehirst, Lord Home, and many more. In the Highlands, it was no doubt statesmanlike to try to govern the western seaboard and the islands by royal agents rather than by local magnates, but by displacing the Earl of Argyll from his position of influence the King made another powerful enemy. Apart from the Borders and the Highlands, James's proceedings show many instances of a solicitude for order and a determination to have the laws obeyed, but the difficulty was to judge where firmness ended and severity began. James was not only severe, he was vindictive, and some of the punishments he imposed suggest a streak of sadistic cruelty in his nature.

It is clear, too, that some of his actions against nobles and others were prompted by motives which had little to do with statesmanship. In the first place, the kin and supporters of Angus, who was himself unpardonable, were perpetually under suspicion. Lady Glamis, a sister of Angus, was put to death by burning on a charge of conspiring against the King, and the Master of Forbes, whose wife was a sister of Angus, was put to death on a charge of plotting to shoot the King. Sometimes the reason for the King's implacable persecution of some notable seems to have been nothing more than a desire for his goods. The son of the Earl of Crawford, known as 'the wicked Master', was compelled, possibly for sound enough reasons, to renounce his succession to the title, but the Earl himself was mulcted in large sums of money on one pretext or another and compelled to mortgage many of his lands to meet the crown's demands. The Earl of Morton, who had no male heir, was relentlessly harried by the King until he agreed to resign his lands (under protest that he did so in fear of death)—an act of manifest injustice which was reversed after James's death. The mysterious fate of Sir James Hamilton of Finnart shows the same pattern. He had been high in the royal favour as the King's master of works, but was suddenly seized and executed, and it was said that the real reason was the King's wish to annex his property. The fact is that as the years went on James showed more and more signs of acquisitiveness; 'this King inclineth daily more and more to covetousness', an English agent remarked in 1539.

The King's ecclesiastical policy was likewise shaped partly by his acquisitiveness. His own religious views were complex and inconsistent. His private life was scandalous by any standards, yet, like his father, he may have combined his own disregard for any moral law with genuine respect for those whose standards were more austere, and he certainly did commend the Observant Friars, who represented the most vital and strict element in the Church at the time. However, it may not be cynical to remark that the Observants, with their rigid adherence to the rule of poverty, were an inexpensive order. Equally, James practised the traditional devotion to shrines and relics, but he evidently enjoyed the satirical attacks made on them in the verses of Sir David Lindsay, his one-time tutor. Yet again, neither his respect for the Observants nor his appreciation of Lindsay's attacks on the worldliness of many of the clergy led him to favour effective measures for reform. His occasional prosecutions of heretics, on the other hand, merely represented the orthodoxy which the pope had purchased when he permitted the Scottish King to tax the Church. The bargain with the papacy extended far beyond taxation, for the pope, faced with the defection of England, was resolved to retain the allegiance of Scotland even at the cost of almost abdicating his authority in that country, and he conceded to King James the full right of nominating the holders of Scottish bishoprics and abbeys. James, like his father, consulted only his own interests and those of favoured noble families when he made appointments to high office in the Church. His ecclesiastical policy as a whole, in so far as the price paid for his orthodoxy meant that he had a free hand to despoil the Church and to appoint unworthy prelates, did much to weaken the ecclesiastical system.

How strong heresy may have become in James's reign is hard to determine, and it would be equally hard to disentangle those who were unorthodox in doctrine from those who wished merely to revive ecclesiastical discipline and from those who wished to follow Henry VIII's example of breaking with Rome and so align Scotland with England. Henry did his best to publicise in Scotland the benefits which accrued to the crown from the dissolution of the monasteries, but so far as James was concerned English example had no attractions, as he was making enough out of the Church, with full papal approval, and had no need to proceed to any revolutionary measures. However, while the price paid by the Church was enough to secure James's orthodoxy, his subjects may not have seen things as he did. There are some indications that a number of noble and lairdly families, especially in Fife, Angus and Ayrshire, had already committed themselves to a pro-English and reforming policy to which they were in future to adhere consistently. There is, therefore, nothing improbable in the allusions made by more than one contemporary to a 'black list' of 350 nobles and barons whose estates might be confiscated should the King choose to institute proceedings against them for heresy. If anything like that number of prominent and influential people felt that they were thus in the King's hands, his position must have been precarious indeed.

James's acquisitiveness, which coloured so many of his actions, was in itself successful. Owing to the confiscations of lands from the many nobles and others who were prosecuted for one reason or another, the crown's income from land rose spectacularly in the later years of the reign. Equally, other proceedings against malefactors or disaffected persons brought in revenues in fines and in the sums paid for pardons. James's marriages brought him two dowries—100,000 gold crowns with Madeleine, 100,000 francs and an annuity of 20,000 francs with Mary,* and stores of plate, clothing and jewels in addition. The levies on the Church, through the three tenths and the composition for the 'Great Tax', represented very large sums. Besides, the King's illegitimate sons, as infants, were appointed commendators of the wealthy religious houses of Melrose, Kelso, St Andrews, Coldingham and Holyrood, and the fruits of those establishments also came into the royal coffers.

James spent a lot, too. He left some of the finest Scottish secular building, especially at Falkland, Stirling and Linlithgow. An expedition which he led to the Isles in 1540 was equipped in a luxurious style, and his household had a huge staff. It was perhaps characteristic that he repeatedly spent money on improving and adorning the regalia, and he was responsible for the fashioning of the Scottish crown as it is now to be seen in Edinburgh Castle. Yet James also hoarded a large proportion of his income. One contemporary put his fortune at his death at 300,000 livres, and if the figure is correct it would suggest that little of the capital value of the Queens' dowries had ever been spent. Even the record evidence that in Edinburgh Castle alone he left a sum of at least 20,000 merks (£13,333 13*s.* 4*d.*) is sufficiently impressive

*1 crown = 2·25 livres or francs

when we recall the state of bankruptcy in which he had found the national finances. His hoarding can hardly have endeared him to his subjects, and his ambitious building, though it may have been popular with those to whom it gave employment, was criticised as being more sumptuous than the country could afford.

James's nature was such that he is unlikely to have made a deliberate attempt to conciliate any section of the community. It is true that his parliaments confirmed many old acts, and passed new ones, which were designed to be beneficial to the generality of the people, but it would be hard to see any proof of a deliberate bid for popular support, and his exactions from the Church had the indirect effect of worsening the condition of the tenants on the ecclesiastical estates. It may be that his severity against malefactors and his insistence on respect for the law won him the favour of the law-abiding, but it would be dangerous to argue that this had been his intention. James lives in some contemporary tales and in popular tradition as a 'poor man's king', who loved to wander about among his subjects in disguise—a habit immortalised by Sir Walter Scott in *The Lady of the Lake*. But this may have sprung not from any policy but from a taste for low company which he had acquired during his minority. It may have been the same taste, as well as his distrust of the nobility, which led him to rely on men of middle-class origins. And, while this gave him some competent servants and was continuing a tradition established when Angus had alienated the nobility and so had of necessity given an unusual opportunity to lesser men, it involved the fatal error of slighting the nobility as James III had done.

No Scottish king could have pursued the policies of James V without alienating many of his subjects, and there are signs of disaffection from as early as 1531 onwards. Taking into account his vindictiveness, his ruthlessness and his cruelty, as well as his acquisitiveness, he must have been one of the most unpopular monarchs who ever sat on the Scottish throne. 'So sore a dread king', it was reported in 1537, 'and so ill beloved of his subjects, was never in that land: every man that hath any substance fearing to have a quarrel made to begin therefor.'

This state of mind among the people of Scotland was a poor foundation for a foreign policy which involved military operations in which the King's subjects were expected to take part. In 1538 and 1539 it seemed for a time that the great crusade against the schismatic Henry VIII, long envisaged by the pope, was at last to take shape, because Francis of France and the Emperor Charles were for a brief space at peace, and the pope, who had already been proclaiming a general council to rally the Roman Catholic powers around him, now ordered the execution of a bull excommunicating Henry. But the coalition soon dissolved. By 1541 Francis and Charles were again at loggerheads, and, far from being ready to combine against Henry, were each seeking his aid. When Scotland, faithful to her engagements to France and Rome, sent David Beaton to France to ask for help against England, France declined to comply. Scotland, in fact, was the only partner in the supposed crusade who was prepared to act, and all that came of the grand design was an Anglo-Scottish war in which Scotland was unaided.

England, under the threat of attack from the Continent, had tried to ensure the neutrality or support of Scotland. Henry's persuasive tactics, designed to make James follow his example in ecclesiastical policy, were successful to the extent that James agreed to meet the English King at York. But the Scottish council declined to let their King leave the country. There were good enough grounds for refusing, because Henry had often contemplated the kidnapping of James, even on Scottish soil, and the King's person was especially precious as two sons born to his Queen had recently died. But the real obstacle to the meeting, it was alleged, was the attitude of the Scottish clergy, who feared that James would be persuaded to imitate English example. Scotland, in short, was not only unaided by other powers when she confronted England. She was also divided. While the prelates, and ecclesiastical conservatives generally, adhered to the French alliance and supported a campaign against England, there were many who took a different view. James was to find, as Albany had done, that the Scottish nobles would not cross the Border, but their hesitation now had a religious as well as a political motive: in their eyes, Scotland was now adventuring on behalf of the papacy, just as in 1513 she had adventured on behalf of France.

Henry, who—for the only time in his life—made the long journey to York, and made it in vain, was indignant when James did not appear, and he proceeded to reassert old English claims to superiority over Scotland. An English force which crossed the Border was worsted at Haddon Rig, but even this success did not make the Scottish magnates ready to invade England. The King charged them with being faint-hearted, and there was complete estrangement between the monarch and his nobles. They were excluded from the counsels of the King, who resigned the direction of affairs to Cardinal Beaton and to Oliver Sinclair. The latter, though not of low birth, ranks as the last of James's 'minions' or unpopular favourites.

In the actual battle at Solway Moss, Scottish Borderers turned on their own fellow countrymen, seized some of the nobles and handed them over to the English. Lord Maxwell, one of the Borderers who had fallen foul of the King, was reported to have deliberately instigated the confusion which made the battle a disastrous rout. Some nobles seem to have surrendered without striking a blow. James's policy had resulted in disaffection among the Borderers and in a preference for being taken prisoner by the English rather than dying in the service of a King in whom so many of his subjects had completely lost confidence.

James V is described by some contemporary or near-contemporary writers as strong and courageous in body and spirit. Yet the disaster and disgrace of Solway Moss was followed by rapid and complete collapse. The battle was fought on 24 November, and on 14 December the King died. He had retired to Edinburgh, Linlithgow (where he spent a week with his Queen) and then Falkland. He had no will to live, and declined to make any arrangements for keeping Christmas, because, as he said, by that time the realm would be masterless. Yet there is no evidence of bodily illness, and his collapse seems to have been one of spirit and mind rather than of body. The causes were partly personal. He had lost his first wife, and when the two sons born to his second wife died within a few days of each other in 1541 he was plunged into depression. The prospective failure of legitimate issue was a sharp contrast to the health of his bastard brood. Then Solway Moss, besides being a disaster for his foreign policy and a revelation of his failure at home, involved also the disgrace of his favourite Oliver Sinclair. To judge from contemporary reports, in his last hours James reviewed in his mind the errors of his policy in exiling Angus, forfeiting nobles and imprisoning men who might have served him better than those he had lately been employing. But, according to the more picturesque narrators, his regrets were as much personal as political. They tell how he moancd, 'Fy, fled Oliver? Is Oliver tane? All his lost'; how he received the news of his daughter's birth with the words, 'It came with a lass, it will pass with a lass'; and how he turned his back to his lords and his face to the wall.

35 James V
From a woodcut of 1541

9 ♛

Mary, Queen of Scots, 1542-67

The history of Scotland during Mary's minority, and the events of her own early life, were determined by the situation which had taken shape in the later years of her father's reign. Scotland, divided internally between the friends of England and of the Reformation on one side and the friends of France and the papacy on the other, was subjected to pressures from outside as France and England each sought, sometimes by war and sometimes by diplomacy, to turn Scotland into a satellite.

The new Queen, born at Linlithgow on 8 December 1542, was hardly a week old when her father died. Her person remained, inevitably, in the custody of her mother, Mary of Guise, but there seems to have been no thought of repeating earlier practice and investing the Queen Mother with political power as well. In this minority, for the first time since that of James I, there was present in the country an heir presumptive of mature years, and to him were assigned the offices of tutor of the Queen and of Governor of the realm. He was James Hamilton, second Earl of Arran, a grandson of Mary, daughter of James II, who had married Lord Hamilton. Arran was the most irresolute of men, and, with no policy of his own—save perhaps the interests of his house—he was peculiarly open to the influence of stronger characters.

The English interest was the first to gain ascendancy, for Henry VIII intervened now with far greater effect than he had ever been able to do in James V's reign. He sent for Angus, the veteran leader of the anglophile faction among the Scots, who had been an exile in England since 1528, and groomed him for a resumption of his old rôle. Henry had also at his disposal a number of lords who had been captured at Solway Moss and were prepared to earn their liberation by undertaking to further the English cause in Scotland. When Angus and those 'English lords', as they were called, arrived in Scotland they established a domination over Arran and gained control of affairs. Cardinal Beaton, leader of the conservative and pro-French party, was imprisoned, a parliament followed English advice to 'let slip the Bible' among the people of Scotland, and negotiations were begun for the marriage of the infant Queen to Prince Edward of England, afterwards Edward VI, now six years of age. The Treaties of Greenwich, providing for peace between England and Scotland during the reigns of Henry and Mary and for the betrothal of Mary to Edward, were drawn up in July 1543 and ratified by Arran in August.

But before the year was out the Scots had repudiated the treaties and had renewed the league with France. There were several reasons for the *volte-face*. Arran, although his name had headed the 'black list' of heretics in the previous reign and he now announced that for years he had considered the pope to be no more than a bishop 'and that a very evil bishop', had no conscientious attachment to the cause of Reformation. He had been alarmed by Henry's demands that Mary should be taken to England before she was of marriageable age, and his anxiety had been only partly allayed by the Treaties of Greenwich, according to which she was to leave Scotland when she was ten. He saw that if Henry once had Mary in his hands his own reversionary right to the throne might be nullified, whereas, if Mary remained in Scotland and did not marry Edward, she might be united to his own son and heir, the Master of Hamilton. Besides, Arran was conscious of a certain insecurity in his own position as heir presumptive, for his legitimacy was not above reproach, and he had been presented with an object lesson in the spring of 1543, when

Matthew, Earl of Lennox, who was next in the line of succession after him, arrived from France. This was a reminder that Arran was wholly at the mercy of the Church, which, as the judge in matrimonial cases, could confirm or deny the legality of his parents' marriage. Arran was thus peculiarly susceptible to the influence of Cardinal Beaton, head of the hierarchy in Scotland, who regained his liberty in the summer and renewed clerical opposition to the English alliance. Arran was, in addition, much influenced by another churchman, his brother John, Abbot of Paisley, who had returned from the Continent in the spring. A much abler man than the Governor, and for many years the effective head of the house of Hamilton, Abbot John had a clear-sighted grasp of his family's interest which reinforced his professional connection with the pro-French party. At one stage it was remarked of the Governor that 'what the English lords decide him to do one day, the Abbot changes the next'. The French cause, therefore, had its supporters, no less than the English, and France was also active directly, for she sent money and munitions to encourage Scottish resistance to England.

Henry had played into the hands of his opponents, for he had aroused suspicion by his eagerness to see Mary on his side of the Border, he had not ratified the Treaties of Greenwich within the prescribed period of two months, and he seized some Scottish ships which had put to sea trusting that the formulation of the Treaties involved abstinence from war. Yet, when the Scots went back on their bargain, Henry was a very angry man. Instinctively, he turned to a policy of force. In 1544 and again in 1545, English armies invaded the south of Scotland, with instructions to do the maximum amount of damage to Scottish property in buildings, movable goods, crops and herds. The effect of this policy of frightfulness was not to foster affection in Scotland for either England or the Reformation. Nor was Henry very successful in his efforts to tamper with the allegiance of the Scottish magnates by means of bribery. True, they accepted English pensions: but they accepted pensions from the Scottish government and the French government as well, and on the whole did rather less service to England than to their other employers. Henry did gain the consistent support of the Earl of Lennox, who invariably took the opposite side from his dynastic rival, Arran, but hardly any other Scottish noble could be relied on for English ends. The short-term effect of Henry's proceedings was in the main to strengthen the position of Arran, who came to be associated in a kind of coalition with Cardinal Beaton and Mary of Guise, and there was so much patriotic repugnance to the marriage of the Queen to an English prince that a growing number of Scots came to favour her betrothal to Arran's son.

Henry did, however, see two things clearly. One was that the English interest in Scotland could be effectively fostered by encouraging the spread of reforming ideas. The other point in which his judgment was not at fault was in discerning Cardinal Beaton as the main obstacle to the English cause. In 1544 the English invaders had received special instructions to 'turn the Cardinal's town of St Andrews upside down, leaving not one stone upon another', and from that point Henry engaged in more than one plot for the assassination of Beaton. It is not altogether clear that the conspiracy which ultimately resulted in Beaton's murder, in 1546, was directly of Henry's making, but the elimination of the Cardinal was a success for the friends of England, and the murderers seized the castle of St Andrews and appealed for English help. England did not intervene in time to save them, for St Andrews fell to a French expedition in the summer of 1547, but she replied to French intervention by sending north the last of a long series of great invading armies. Henry had died in January, and the Protector of England under the young Edward VI was the Duke of Somerset, who, as Earl of Hertford, had harried Scotland in 1544 and 1545. In September 1547 he routed the Scots with heavy losses, at Pinkie, near Musselburgh. After the battle the English adopted a policy of seizing and fortifying a number of strong points on the Scottish east coast, as far north as the Firth of Tay, and also established a force in Haddington, from which much of the Lothians could be dominated. The aim now was not conquest, or destruction followed by withdrawal, but the permanent, or at any rate prolonged, occupation of limited but important areas.

The Scottish government completely lacked the power to eject the invaders. Arran, deprived of the support of the Cardinal, was manifestly inept. He had mishandled the situation at St Andrews after Beaton's murder, though in truth he had been in a difficult position, as his son, who was in the castle as a kind of hostage for his father's good behaviour, had fallen into the hands of the murderers. But it was not creditable that French help had been necessary to reduce the castle. The Pinkie disaster did further damage to Arran's prestige, and he was also discredited by his blatant pursuance of the financial interests of his kinsmen. Because confidence in him dwindled, the support once extended to the proposed marriage of Mary to the Master of Hamilton was withdrawn. But the incapacity of Arran was not the only factor which weakened the Scots. The results were increasingly apparent of the English policy of making friends by fostering the Reformation, and the English armies of occupation received the countenance of many Scots in whose minds religion outweighed patriotism. One contemporary thoughtfully concluded that the main reason 'why Englishmen are favoured' was that 'part of the lieges have taken new opinions of the scriptures and have done against the law and ordinance of holy church'.

If the English were to be evicted from Scotland, they could be evicted only with French help. And the help was given, but only on conditions. By a treaty concluded in the camp outside the English fortifications at Haddington, it was agreed that Queen Mary, who had at one time been destined to be the bride of the heir to the throne of England, should be sent to France with the prospect of becoming the bride of the heir to the throne of France. In the critical period after Pinkie, the child had been sent for safety to the island priory of Inchmahome, and now, in July 1548, she sailed from Dumbarton for France. At almost the same time, the Master of Hamilton, who had already been a hostage for his father in the hands of Cardinal Beaton and then in the hands of Beaton's murderers, was sent to France, once more in effect as a hostage to ensure the compliance of Arran with French policy. The French side of the agreement made at Haddington was carried out: military help was given in Scotland itself, and pressure on the English forces in France finally compelled England to acknowledge defeat and withdraw her forces from south-eastern Scotland.

But Scotland was to find that she had escaped from an English occupation only to become the victim of a French occupation. For a time, French control was indirect, and French influence was merely insinuated by means which had some regard for Scottish interests and Scottish sentiment. Arran, now endowed with the French duchy of Châtelherault as the reward for his surrender of the Queen and of his son, remained Governor, and his half-brother, the one-time Abbot of Paisley, became Archbishop of St Andrews. Other Scottish notables who might have shown some disposition to maintain the pro-English and reforming cause were judiciously treated; in 1550 they were taken to France by Mary of Guise, so that they might be subjected to indoctrination and exposed to French offers, and the report was that the King of France had 'bought them completely'. It was plain that the Hamiltons, though invested nominally with the headship of Church and State, were unlikely to be able to resist should France bring real pressure to bear, but there were for a time two difficulties in the way of the formal displacement of Arran from the office of Governor. He had been appointed to hold office 'during the Queen's non-age', and tutory lasted, by a well-understood rule, until the 'pupil', if a girl, reached the age of twelve, which Mary would not do until December 1554. Secondly, England under Edward VI had been moving further and further in the direction of Protestantism, and there was a possibility that Arran, if threatened with dispossession, might reverse his earlier *volte-face* and appeal for English help against France 'on the grounds of the religion'.

However, in July 1553 Edward VI died and his sister Mary, who succeeded, soon showed that English ecclesiastical policy was going to be reversed and that England would no longer support a Protestant movement in Scotland. And in December 1553, when Mary was *entering* her twelfth year, an opinion was obtained in Paris that she was now of age to choose her own curator in place of a tutor, and so to dispose of the regency. The Scots did not accept this interpretation of the law, and even after it was pronounced the French did not venture on a forcible dispossession of Arran. Instead, he was induced to resign his office, in return for an undertaking that no questions would be asked about his dealings in crown property during his governorship, and in April 1554 he was replaced by Mary of Guise.

From this point, action was taken in Scotland which was openly designed to serve the interests of French foreign policy. France soon found herself at war with Spain and with England (which were linked through the marriage of Mary Tudor with Philip II) and it was of some importance to her to be able to use Scotland as a base to threaten England from the rear. For a time the war went much against France, but in its later stages she took the offensive, and by 1558 there was a clear intention to combine a movement against England's only remaining possession in France—Calais—with an attack on Berwick-on-Tweed, England's sole possession in Scotland and the other remaining fruit of all England's medieval wars. By this time Berwick had not been in Scottish hands for nearly eighty years, and the prospect of regaining it was no inducement to the Scots. The operations which the French proposed were, in short, patently aggressive, and, far from creating enthusiasm in Scotland, encountered bitter opposition. Experience on many occasions in the past had shown that, however attractive the 'auld alliance' might be as a weapon against England, yet when Frenchmen came to Scotland, at least in any numbers, there was certain to be friction with the Scots. At this stage, under a French Queen Regent, there was a French resident who shared power and prestige with her, Frenchmen were thrust into offices in the administration, and French forces garrisoned Scottish fortresses like Dunbar, Inchkeith and Leith. As the numbers of French troops increased, and their wives and families came to join them and settle in Scotland, criticism fastened on the prospect that native Scots would be ousted from their farms and estates in favour of those strangers. The number of French troops probably never rose as high as 4,000, but they were trained professional soldiers who startled a country where a standing army had been unknown, and they would clearly be an effective force against any untried native levies should the Scots attempt resistance. At the same time, if there were to be large-scale operations against England, a Scottish army would have to be enlisted, and any such proposal was bound to encounter the refusal of the Scots, persistent since Flodden, to invade England in the service of France. The government preferred, instead of the traditional 'host' or general muster, an army of 'wagers' or mercenaries. But they would have to be paid. The Scots had not yet become habituated to taxation of any kind, and what was proposed at this stage was something almost unbelievably far-reaching in its incidence. The suggestion was made to the estates that a kind of census of all the men in the country should be compiled, with a valuation of their possessions in both heritable and movable property. This astounding proposal was rejected, and various other taxes which were imposed were paid only with 'murmurings' and 'grudges'.

It was therefore in an atmosphere of suspicion that the marriage of Queen Mary to the Dauphin Francis was celebrated in the cathedral of Notre Dame in Paris on 24 April 1558. Publicly, provisions were made to preserve the integrity of the Scottish kingdom and to safeguard the rights of the native heirs to the throne in the event of Mary's death without issue. But by secret instruments Mary in effect signed away her kingdom to the French, and the belief in France was that the sovereignty of Scotland had, quite simply, been transferred to the French royal house. Even if contemporaries in Scotland were not aware of Mary's duplicity and of French attitudes, they saw a bleak prospect for their country. They did not know, as we do, that Francis would die in less than three years, leaving Mary a childless widow. The likelihood was that he would live, that Mary and he would have children, and that their descendants would rule both

France and Scotland. In such circumstances, it was acutely observed, Scotland was likely to be absorbed into France, just as Brittany had been absorbed earlier in the century through the marriage of Brittany's heiress, the Duchess Anne, to the French King.

Patriotic resentment against French domination might of itself have in time provoked rebellion. But before a crisis came that resentment was reinforced by the emergence of a revolutionary attitude among ecclesiastical reformers, and when a revolt broke out it was one in which it is hard to disentangle political from religious aims and motives.

Ever since the Lutheran Reformation began to influence the east coast burghs and their hinterland in the 1520s, the circulation of Protestant teaching of one kind or another had been continuous. The evidence is to be found in occasional prosecutions for heresy, in intermittent outbreaks of iconoclasm and spoliation of ecclesiastical property, and in dealings in church revenues which strongly suggest that the clergy were aware that a crisis was approaching. On the other side, there were various reasons why the authority which should have suppressed attacks on the Church was ineffective. Probably ecclesiastical discipline generally had never recovered from the shock it had sustained in 1543, when the government's decision to release the vernacular Bible had been the signal for radical elements to become vocal and militant. In succeeding years, the English invasions of 1544 and 1545 did no good to either the fabric or the community life of the religious houses in the south-east. In 1546 Cardinal Beaton's murder was again a signal for attacks on ecclesiastical properties, and from 1547 to 1549 there was another phase of destructive military operations. In the last years of Châtelherault's governorship, when stability of a kind was returning, Archbishop Hamilton summoned two councils of the Church which passed a whole code of statutes designed to curb abuses like concubinage, nonresidence and pluralism and to raise the intellectual as well as the moral standards of the clergy. But such measures may have encouraged the Protestant preachers to believe that the authorities might concede still more if they were further pressed, and Hamilton was too wary to risk unpopularity by taking strong action against the reformers. When Châtelherault was superseded as Governor by Mary of Guise in 1554, the administration again had reasons for refraining from energetic measures against the Protestants. For one thing, leniency towards them might help to offset the discontent caused by the pro-French policy. Besides, if Protestant preachers had liberty in Scotland they might encourage the English Protestants who sought to undermine the government of Mary Tudor. And, in any event, as long as Mary Tudor reigned in England, there was no danger that a Protestant revolt in Scotland could count on assistance from the English government. All in all, therefore, the Scottish reformers enjoyed a degree of liberty which enabled them to spread their teaching and even develop an organisation.

The situation changed dramatically at the end of 1558. Elizabeth Tudor succeeded her sister in November, and as soon as it became evident that England was likely once more to throw off allegiance to Rome there were signs that the Scottish opposition would welcome English help against the French army of occupation. Besides, the Scottish reformers, encouraged by the prospects opened up by the new reign in England, showed a new militancy when, at the beginning of 1559, they formally threatened the friars with dispossession at the next Whitsunday term. While the Scottish opposition, both political and ecclesiastical, was thus on the move, the Scottish government was presently in a position to take up its challenge with a new resolution. Ever since the negotiations associated with Queen Mary's marriage had been successfully concluded, there had been less need to woo the Scots into acquiescence in French policy, and the increasing success of French arms on the Continent, culminating in the capture of Calais in January 1558, had made it less likely that France would have to try to induce the Scots to fight on England's northern frontier. Then, in the spring of 1559, when France and Spain made peace, France was free to turn on the Protestants within her own territory and Mary of Guise was stimulated to pursue the same policy in Scotland, as part of a kind of united front against those who were disaffected to the Church.

When the Queen Regent summoned Protestant preachers to answer for their disobedience to authority, she found that their lay friends were prepared to support them, and forces were mustered on both sides. John Knox, who had previously been active in Scotland for only brief periods, returned from Geneva in May 1559 and incited attacks on religious houses which coincided with the term at which the friars had been told to quit. The insurgents, gathering strength, were able to move south from Perth, where the trouble had started, and even to occupy Edinburgh, while the French withdrew to Dunbar.

It soon became apparent that the untrained and unpaid forces of the insurgents could not keep the field for long, and the Regent, with a professional army, was not going to be coerced into altering her policy or relinquishing power. Appeals were made for English help, but Elizabeth, uncertain as yet of the strength of her own position, was unwilling to countenance rebellion in a neighbouring country and against another Queen, and she thought that she could not afford armed intervention. The Scots therefore sought to strengthen their position by setting up a substitute for their absent Queen, and were perhaps the more ready to do so because in July 1559 she had become Queen of France and the government of Scotland was carried on in the names of 'Francis and Mary, King and Queen of France and Scotland'. Mary's half-brother, the Lord James Stewart, was one possible candidate for the throne, but no illegitimate son of a monarch had been raised to the throne within historic times, and there was clearly more to be said for the Duke of Châtelherault, who was legally heir presumptive, although his ability, as his past record showed, was far inferior to that of Lord James. Châtelherault, however, was not a free agent, for his son, so long a hostage for his father, was still in France under surveillance. Then, through English agency, young Arran was enabled to escape, and he reached Scotland in September 1559. His father immediately joined the insurgents as their titular head, and in

October it was declared that authority was transferred from Mary of Guise to a great council of the realm, under the Duke's presidency.

This political change did little to strengthen either the military or the financial position of the insurgents, and the end of 1559 saw their forces driven back in disorder from Edinburgh, while the soldiers of the Queen Regent were secure in Leith behind fortifications which had been rendered impregnable against any artillery the reformers could muster, and there they could await reinforcements from France. English help was more urgently required than ever. Elizabeth's initial intervention, in January 1560, took the shape of a naval expedition which cut Leith off from the hope of reinforcements and also interrupted the operations which the French troops were carrying on successfully against the insurgents in Fife. After a formal agreement had been made which pledged England to eject the French from Scotland, an English army entered Scotland at the end of March. Leith was closely invested and battered by artillery, but the defenders put up a tenacious resistance even when they were reduced to famine. The French government, however, decided not to continue the struggle, and the way to a settlement was eased by the death, on 11 June, of the gallant Queen Regent, who had endured so much for her country, her Church and her daughter's rights.

By the Treaty of Edinburgh (July 1560), both English and French troops were to withdraw from Scotland, leaving the Scots free to settle their own affairs. This they did, but along lines which might have seemed inconceivable a few months earlier. It had become very clear that the proposal to transfer the crown from Mary, even to the heir presumptive, made far less appeal than the cause of a religious Reformation, let alone the cause of national independence against the French. Therefore, partly in order to win more general support, but partly to meet Elizabeth's preference for the maintenance of her sister Queen's rights, the proposed political revolution had been quietly dropped. A parliament which met in August was held in the names of Mary and Francis. Its legislation involved no political change, and was silent even on ecclesiastical polity and endowment—which were likewise controversial subjects—but concentrated on the abolition of papal authority, the prohibition of the celebration of mass and the adoption of a reformed Confession of Faith.

Yet those who still hankered after a political change were encouraged by the continued absence of Queen Mary, and the likelihood that she would remain in France rather than return to a Scotland which had decisively rejected France and much that France stood for. Her life for a dozen years and more, almost as long as she could remember, had been shaped by her position in France, first as prospective bride of the Dauphin, then as Dauphiness, and finally, since July 1559, as Queen of France. Her own ancient kingdom, by contrast, offered her little or nothing in comparison. Should Mary not return, and should she perhaps voluntarily abdicate, Châtelherault would certainly be King, and his son would be heir apparent. And the faction which looked forward to this had it in mind to secure the Reformation in Scotland and a lasting settlement with England by marrying young Arran to Queen Elizabeth.

The situation changed suddenly in December 1560, when Francis II died. Mary was now nothing more in France than a dowager, and at court she was overshadowed by the Queen Mother, the masterful Catharine de' Medici—who, oddly enough, had at one time been a possible bride of Mary's father. Charles IX, who succeeded Francis, was a boy of eleven, and his mother gained power, while Mary's family, the Guises, were excluded from political influence. It was at once realised that Mary was now likely to be thrown back on Scotland.

It was thought, too, that should Mary return her next husband might well be the young Earl of Arran, until now the suitor of Queen Elizabeth. There were both personal and political reasons for this scheme. It had not been forgotten that in 1544–6, when old Arran was guided by Cardinal Beaton, considerable support had been secured for the betrothal of his son to the Queen. The Cardinal's murder, and the subsequent intervention of the French in Scotland, had put an end to the project as a political one.

But the children had both been taken to France in 1548. There they saw something of each other, and apparently there was a kind of 'boy and girl affair' as a result of which Arran was led to understand that if any hitch occurred in the arrangements between Mary and the Dauphin he could expect to be considered as a future husband. He was in possession of a ring which he believed to be a token of Mary's pledge, and when he heard of the death of Francis he lost no time in sending her the ring to remind her of her promise. This was all purely personal. But the politicians who looked to the maintenance of the Reformation in Scotland and to the preservation of the new Anglo-Scottish amity saw additional advantages in the match, while those who had previously thought in terms of the supersession of Mary by the Hamiltons now saw a way to preserve the lawful monarchy but at the same time secure real power to themselves. Elizabeth rejected Arran's suit for her own hand, and was clearly of opinion that should he marry Mary the Scottish Queen would be shepherded into accepting the Reformation and renouncing the French alliance.

There were others in Scotland who were not anxious either to advance the house of Hamilton or to constrain their Queen in matrimony or religion, and Mary was made aware of the existence of this more moderate party. Consequently, when she left France for Scotland in August 1561, her galleys evaded English ships which may have been designed to drive her to take the western seas to Dumbarton, where the Hamiltons were waiting for her, and they made a dash through timely fogs to Leith, where she was received by the leaders of the moderates—the Lord James Stewart and William Maitland of Lethington, the secretary of state. The wretched Arran, whose hopes of marrying the Queen had become an obsession, soon showed signs of mental instability, and in 1562 his condition was such that he had to be placed in confinement, in which he remained until his death in 1609. Thus Châtelherault, head of the house of Hamilton, 'in the end not only lost his game, but lost it in a manner pitiable almost beyond words'.*

*T. F. Henderson, *Mary, Queen of Scots*, i, 231

Under the guidance of the Lord James (created Earl of Moray in 1562) and Lethington, Mary pursued a policy marked by high political intelligence. The general design was to present her as all things to all men—that is, to conciliate the Scottish Protestants and commend her to Elizabeth for recognition as heir to the English throne, but at the same time to keep alive the hopes of English Roman Catholics who might prefer her to Elizabeth and to maintain communications with the pope and with continental Roman Catholic powers. Thus, on the one hand, Mary reassured the pope with fair words, she insisted on having mass in her own chapel, and she did not ratify the acts of the Parliament of 1560 against the mass and in favour of the reformed religion. On the other hand, she several times issued a proclamation in virtue of which priests were prosecuted and imprisoned for saying mass beyond the confines of the court, she acquiesced in an arrangement whereby a proportion of the wealth of the old Church was shared between the crown and the Protestant ministers, and she consented to legislation which implied the official recognition, though not the full establishment, of the Reformed Church.

While she pursued these policies, Mary was following the line of conciliation, in the tradition of wiser Scottish monarchs. It was also to her advantage that she was a young Queen who had peculiar opportunities in a country where a royal court centred on a sovereign of adult years had been unknown since 1542. She had an attractive, possibly fascinating, personality, and her tall, athletic figure, combined with her liking for open-air activities, must have won her the affections of her people on her many progresses through the country. Each year from 1562 to 1566 she was in Fife in the spring, in 1562 and 1564 she was in Aberdeen and Inverness in the summer, in the summer of 1563 she was in Argyll and Ayrshire, and in the autumns of 1565 and 1566 she was in the south-west or south. Her principal residence was Holyrood, but she spent some quite long periods at Stirling. There would seem to be little doubt that both by policy and personality she made herself acceptable to the great majority of her people. The leading irreconcilable was John Knox, who made up his mind when he first met her that she was 'indurate against God and his truth'. It was caustically observed that he was as full of distrust of the Queen as if he were 'of God's privy council' and knew her destiny. But not even all the ministers, let alone the laymen, of his Church, agreed with him, and many saw no fault in their Queen's policy.

That the happiness of Mary and her subjects was not enduring was not the result of anything that happened within Scotland itself. It was the result of the attitude of Queen Elizabeth. Scottish politicians were all along designing their Queen's policy with an eye at least as much to the English succession as to conciliation in Scotland. Mary's primary bargaining counter was her claim to be not merely Elizabeth's lawful heir presumptive, but the lawful claimant to Elizabeth's throne. Henry VIII's matrimonial adventures had broken all the rules, and in his own lifetime he had bastardised in turn his daughter Mary and his daughter Elizabeth, and it was by a later, arbitrary, decision, rather than by any law or reason, that both Mary and Elizabeth were able to succeed to his throne. In particular, while Roman Catholics recognised Mary Tudor, the daughter of Catharine of Aragon, they could not recognise Elizabeth, the offspring of Henry's union with Anne Boleyn, whom he had married while Catharine was still alive. If Elizabeth was illegitimate, then Mary, Queen of Scots, the granddaughter of Henry VIII's sister, became Queen of England by right of blood on the death of Mary Tudor in 1558. And Mary and Francis had in fact assumed the arms of England in token of their claim—to the indignation of Elizabeth, although she bore on her own shield the lilies of France and styled herself Queen of France. By the Treaty of Edinburgh, in July 1560, it had been agreed that Mary should renounce her use of the English arms, but Mary had declined to ratify the treaty, and with some reason, as its provision for her renunciation of her claim to England 'henceforward' might be taken to exclude her for ever from the English succession. Consequently, Mary's advisers worked for mutual recognition between her and Elizabeth—recognition by Mary of Elizabeth's right to the English throne while she lived, recognition by Elizabeth of Mary's right to succeed. Mary's secondary bargaining counter was, of course, her attitude to the Reformation. Henry IV of France was to declare that Paris was worth a mass, and to Mary London might well be worth an Anglican Communion. Therefore Mary's liberal attitude to the Scottish Reformed Church made a suitable impression in England. On the other hand, her policy was sufficiently equivocal not only to appeal to English Roman Catholics but also to involve a threat that she might come to terms with the pope and with continental Roman Catholic powers and claim Elizabeth's throne as their candidate.

The great obstacle to coming to terms with England lay in Elizabeth's reluctance to recognise Mary or anyone else as her successor and in her refusal to say once and for all whether or not she intended to marry. For a time it seemed likely that the two Queens would actually meet, but in the end it proved impossible to bring Elizabeth to any such decisive action. The obvious Scottish retort was to try the effect of threatening Elizabeth with a marriage between Mary and some continental Roman Catholic, notably Don Carlos, the heir to the Spanish throne. This was a dangerous, and two-edged, move, because, while there was the hope that the danger to England of having the Spaniard on her northern frontier might bring Elizabeth to terms, it was also true that for Mary to marry Don Carlos would assuredly end her prospects of recognition by Elizabeth as heir to the English throne. Yet to Roman Catholic intriguers, marriage with Don Carlos would open the possibility that Mary might be able to obtain Spanish help to gain the English throne by violently ousting Elizabeth and not waiting peacefully for her death in the course of nature. In the end, the negotiations with Don Carlos had to be broken off because that young man became insane.

The continental negotiations do seem to have brought it home to Elizabeth that Mary was determined to find a husband and that it might be to England's advantage to nominate one. The best Elizabeth could do was to make the astounding proposal that Mary should marry Robert Dudley, whom she created Earl of

Leicester—the man with whom Elizabeth herself was thought by many to have a scandalous relationship. Mary's advisers—whatever Mary herself thought—were prepared to countenance even this match if it brought with it a promise of the English succession. But at this point Mary's affairs suddenly ceased to be a matter of politics and began to be ruled not by her head but by her heart.

Mary had a first cousin, Henry Stewart, Lord Darnley. His father, the fourth Earl of Lennox, stood after the Hamiltons in the Scottish succession, and had married the daughter of Margaret Tudor by the Earl of Angus, so that Darnley was next in succession to the English throne after Mary herself. Lennox, after his exploits in Scotland in the 1540s on behalf of Henry VIII, had been forfeited and had lived in England for the better part of twenty years, so that his son, Lord Darnley, was in effect an Englishman. Lennox received permission to return to Scotland in 1564, and was soon followed by Darnley. The possibility of his marrying Mary was not a novel idea, and such a match had much to commend it from the point of view of strengthening Mary's claim to the English succession. Elizabeth chose the moment of Darnley's arrival in Scotland to declare that she had no intention of making any pronouncement about the succession, and this was an intimation that Mary had nothing to gain by trying to please her in matrimony or anything else. But political calculations became unimportant when Mary saw Darnley and took an immediate liking to him as 'the lustiest and best proportionit lang man' that she had seen.

Darnley, though to some extent groomed by his mother to appeal to English Roman Catholic opinion, was not himself at this stage a practising Roman Catholic. Those who described him as 'indifferent in religion' may have been correct, but we do know that, whereas he rarely went to mass, he attended Protestant public worship and used Protestant devotions in private. Mary also took care to allay Protestant apprehensions by reissuing her proclamation against the mass, and the marriage therefore did not involve a departure from the moderate policy she had hitherto pursued. But the marriage was so unpopular that when public proclamation was made that in future the government would be carried on in the names of Henry and Mary, King and Queen of Scots, no one except Lennox, Darnley's father, cried 'God save his Grace'. Protestant agitators could make capital out of the fact that the marriage ceremony was according to the Roman rite; the Lennox family, with its unpatriotic record, cannot have been popular; a marriage into the Lennox family alienated the powerful Hamilton interest; and the marriage meant the displacement from influence of the Earl of Moray, whose policy had collapsed with Elizabeth's refusal to designate Mary as her successor. Moray and Châtelherault therefore raised an aimless rebellion, which was energetically suppressed by Mary, who rode in person at the head of her troops, and Moray was driven to take refuge in England, where he found that Elizabeth, who would have applauded his success, had no welcome for a failure.

The course of events in Scotland continued to be shaped by Mary's personal relationships. It did not take her long to see that Darnley was both morally and mentally worthless, and he found that, although he was styled 'King Henry', he was excluded from any share of political power. Besides—perhaps understandably, in view of her recent experience with Moray and Châtelherault—Mary now fell into the fatal error of neglecting the lords and relying on lesser men. Both Darnley and the lords therefore felt that they were being neglected by their Queen, and their resentment centred on David Rizzio, who seemed to have supplanted them in her favour. Rizzio, at first a musician at court, and more recently a secretary for Mary's French affairs, was so constantly in the royal presence that the magnates believed the Italian to have undue political influence with their Queen, while Darnley suspected him of undue familiarity with his wife. Hostility to Rizzio created a ground for a coalition between Darnley and the lords, who pledged themselves to join in murdering the secretary and in securing for Darnley political power and the 'crown matrimonial', which would have given the succession to his heirs had Mary died without issue. The murder of Rizzio in March 1566, carried out with needless brutality in or near the Queen's presence, seems clearly to have been designed to endanger the life of Mary herself and the life of the child of which she was six months pregnant. It may even have been designed to involve the actual murder of Mary, who might easily have been 'accidentally' stabbed in the confusion when the conspirators broke into her tiny supper-chamber to snatch the favourite from her, for only the presence of mind of the Countess of Argyll, who grasped a candle when the table was overturned, prevented the apartment from being plunged into gloom.

Mary showed courage and intelligence. Not only was she unaffected either physically or mentally by her experience, but she set herself to regain Darnley's affections and so detach him from his allies. Moray and his associates, who had been exiled in England since their rebellion in the previous year, were ready to enter Edinburgh on the day after Rizzio's murder and recover power in association with the murderers. But Darnley and Mary rode off from the town together, so frustrating the intention of the conspirators to control Mary through her husband. The plot had completely failed in all its wider intent.

Mary's next step was to divide her enemies by coming to terms with Moray and some of his fellow rebels, as distinct from the murderers of Rizzio, but all her political skill could not now suffice to revive the degree of mutual confidence which the events of earlier years had done so much to create. The birth of Prince James in June 1566, and his baptism by Roman Catholic rites, did nothing to strengthen the Queen's position. Protestants now saw a danger that the country might be saddled with a Roman Catholic dynasty; Mary herself was no longer the only bulwark against an uncertain and disputable succession; and designing politicians could see in the Prince a possible alternative sovereign, who might be removed from his mother's care and brought up as a Protestant. But again Mary's personal relationships became more important than political calculations. Her reconciliation with Darnley after the Rizzio murder had been brief, and before the end of 1566 their estrangement was so complete that some means had clearly to be found of ridding the Queen of her consort. To make matters worse, Mary showed a growing partiality for James Hepburn, Earl of Bothwell, 'a rash and glorious young man'—and a married man—who was, however, one of the most powerful magnates of south-eastern Scotland and was at least conspicuous for his assured loyalty.

The events which followed, culminating in the death of Darnley in February 1567, are among the most fascinating and mysterious in history. There was for a time talk of a divorce between Mary and her husband, and when Mary objected that a divorce—by which she meant a decree of nullity—might make her child illegitimate, attention turned to other methods of removing Darnley. That Mary was aware of schemes for the elimination of her consort is beyond dispute. It seems unlikely, for instance, that she would suddenly have showered financial benefits on the Protestant ministers, as she did at the end of 1566 and the beginning of 1567, had she not been looking for allies in an approaching crisis. It seems probable that her formal restoration of the Archbishop of St Andrews to his jurisdiction (23 December) was designed to enable him to divorce Darnley from his wife and Bothwell from his; and the divorce of Darnley would mean that, once he ceased to be King, violent action could be taken against him without incurring the penalties of treason. To this extent, Mary may have hoped that some means would be found to give a colour of legality to Darnley's death. But at the same time (24 December) she pardoned the murderers of Rizzio, who had never forgiven Darnley for abandoning them after the murder and were thirsting for his blood. A deed of violence by them, with no pretence whatever at legality, would have suited Mary and Bothwell.

But, while Mary clearly knew before the end of 1566 that something was afoot which would probably lead to Darnley's death in suspicious circumstances, it is much less certain that she was a party to his murder in the following February. It seems much more likely that in January she thought that she was pregnant of a child which everyone knew could not be her husband's, and that she must therefore achieve a reconciliation with Darnley as soon as possible. He had fallen ill at Glasgow, and she went there to bring him back to Edinburgh, where she personally supervised his convalescence at Kirk o' Field, a place on the edge of the country and in a much healthier situation than low-lying Holyrood. There she visited him frequently, there she sometimes spent the night in a room below his, and there she was expected to be on the night the murder took place.

However, while Mary was now planning the preservation of Darnley's life, at least for a time, others had different views. The politicians had no desire to see Darnley restored to an ascendancy over the Queen and an influence on public affairs. The Rizzio murderers wanted to remove him, as an act of personal vengeance. And Bothwell, who saw Darnley's life as the obstacle to his own union with Mary, must, if he believed in the Queen's pregnancy, have been more confident than ever that he would achieve his ends by the elimination of Darnley. There were probably, besides, those among the politicians who thought that their future would be more assured if Mary, as well as Darnley, should die and the young Prince become their puppet, while the Rizzio murderers had, at the very least, no special reason for wanting to preserve Mary's life, which they had not hesitated to endanger by their last act of violence. All these real or potential plotters wanted Darnley out of the way, whether with or without his wife. On the other hand, Darnley himself, who now saw little prospect of his restoration to power by lawful means or through the agency of a Scottish faction, had recently shown an unwonted and ostentatious devotion to the mass and may have toyed with the idea of posing as a papalist champion whom continental Roman Catholics would recognise as King if he could encompass the death of his wife, whose own policy had proved so disappointing to zealous papalists.

Amid such complications, the truth about the actual murder is never likely to be discovered. The storing, under Darnley's lodging, of a large quantity of gunpowder, which produced an explosion heavy enough to demolish the whole building, looks as if it had been planned with the intention of destroying a large number of people, such as Mary and her retinue. On this view, the powder might have been placed there by conspirators who intended to dispose of both Darnley and Mary, or it might have been placed there on Darnley's instructions in order to eliminate his wife and those who influenced her. But the idea of producing a great explosion may have been designed, more subtly, to put it beyond any doubt that the death of Darnley was not an accident, and so draw suspicion on Bothwell and Mary. However, despite contemporary statements that Darnley was 'blawn up wi' pooder', he did not die in the explosion, but was found smothered in the garden. Did the murderers take him out to kill him and then find that, as the powder-train was burning too quickly, they had no time to restore the body to the house? Was he killed in attempting to escape from attackers? Or did he awake to the smell of burning from some accidental fire, and, knowing of the gunpowder which had been introduced by his own agents, flee for his life, only to encounter some of the Rizzio murderers who just happened to be passing through the garden and took the opportunity to despatch him? We shall never know the answers to those questions.

Mary's plan to resume marital relations with her husband—which she had promised to do on the very next night—was shattered, and her only hope of escaping shame was to marry her lover Bothwell. But there was to be no escape from shame, because Bothwell was universally believed to have been responsible for the murder of the King. With almost indecent haste, Bothwell was formally acquitted of guilt by a travesty of justice, and then, by two concurrent and obviously collusive processes, Bothwell and his wife divorced each other—she on the ground of his adultery, he on the ground of consanguinity. Mary's sole concession to respectability was to make a show of yielding to Bothwell by force, when he waylaid her and carried her off to his castle of Dunbar. Their marriage, on 15 May, was by Protestant rites, and in the previous month Mary had formally taken the

Reformed Church under her protection. She had thus thrown away her reputation, shown her approval (if nothing more) of her husband's murder and abandoned the Church of her fathers.

Bothwell had played his game for his own hand, and he had few reliable supporters. It did not take long to form a confederacy of magnates, with the ostensible objects of liberating the Queen from Bothwell and preserving the person of the Prince, but in reality aimed at the transfer of political power to a group of notables and possibly, even from the outset, at the supersession of Mary. Mary and Bothwell encountered the confederate lords at Carberry, and the Queen, without bloodshed, surrendered, while Bothwell made his escape. Mary, worn-out and travel-stained, unsuitably clad and—for a time—broken in spirit and distracted, was brought into Edinburgh in disgrace, to be insulted by crowds who shouted 'Burn the whore'. Within forty-eight hours of the surrender she was hustled off to the island castle of Lochleven, where on 24 July she was compelled to abdicate in favour of her son. While at Lochleven, Mary miscarried of twins who had certainly been conceived before the marriage to Bothwell and very probably before the death of Darnley.

The revolution of 1567 was something unprecedented in the history of Scottish kingship. The mere fact of successful rebellion was unusual enough, but the deposition of a sovereign by subjects had not been paralleled since the times of misty antiquity. It is true that James III had been overthrown at Sauchieburn, but he had conveniently been killed immediately afterwards, so that the problem of superseding him by his son with some show of legality did not arise. It was something new for a faction to imprison their sovereign, extort an abdication, and proclaim the heir as King. Consequently, while there had been massive support for a rising designed to 'liberate' Mary from Bothwell, it was shown again now, as it had been in 1560, that there was far more hesitation about any transference of authority from the lawful sovereign. Comparatively few were in favour of Mary's imprisonment and her compulsory abdication.

Just how strong a party Mary's cause could attract was shown when, on 2 May 1568, she escaped from Lochleven. Within a very few days, no fewer than nine earls, nine bishops, twelve commendators and eighteen lords rallied round her, and a force of some 5,000 or 6,000 men was raised. It was, however, outgeneralled by the King's party and defeated at Langside (13 May). Mary fled towards the Solway and crossed to England on 16 May. The history of the eleven days after she left Lochleven is not the least instructive passage in her whole career, and indeed in the history of the Scottish monarchy. No doubt the pitiable tale of her misfortunes as a woman aroused sympathy, and no doubt some who found that they enjoyed less influence under the new régime than they had expected were ready now to attempt to overthrow the regency. But that Mary, after the ineptitude she had displayed in the last year or two, and after the shame and disgrace she had incurred, could command so much support, would seem to be at once significant of the attachment to the lawful sovereign and creditable to her own record in earlier years. Had she never decided, as she did in 1565, to let her heart rule her head, she might have had a long and successful reign and died secure in the affections of her subjects.

36 James VI, at the age of 14
From a woodcut of 1580

10

The Achievement of James VI, 1567–1625

James VI was not the last King to be crowned in Scotland, for Charles I was crowned at Holyrood in 1633 and Charles II at Scone in 1651, but his coronation had significant features which make it almost as worthy of examination as that of Alexander III nearly 300 years before. The new King had attained the throne as a result of a revolution which deposed his predecessor and left her still alive, though in captivity, and this was something that had not happened since Edgar superseded Donald Bane in 1097. His title was the more precarious in that comparatively few of those who had been prepared to join in a confederacy to liberate Mary from Bothwell were ready to acquiesce in the imprisonment of the Queen, her forced abdication and the coronation of her son. No more than five earls and eight lords are named as being present when James was crowned on 29 July 1567.

Plainly, the utmost care had to be taken to arrange a coronation which conformed to precedent. On the other hand, the coronation was the first since the Reformation, and the King's supporters took their stand on the religious changes proclaimed by the Parliament of 1560—the abolition of papal authority, the prohibition of the mass and the adoption of a reformed Confession of Faith. It was thus necessary to marry the traditional features of a coronation with recognition of a novel ecclesiastical situation. Even the scene of the coronation may have had its significance. Like his mother, James was crowned at Stirling; she had been crowned in the chapel royal in the Castle, but that building was suffering from neglect, and in any event the reformers laid their emphasis on parish churches as places of worship, so James was crowned in the church of the Holy Rude, the parish church of Stirling, which presents its spectacular three-sided apse on the steep approach from the town to the castle.

It may be that consideration was given to the possibility that the crown might be placed on the infant monarch's head by one of those nobles who were in truth bestowing the crown which they had taken from his mother, just as in 1651 the crown was to be placed on the head of Charles II by the Marquis of Argyll, and there may have been antiquaries who recalled the place once taken by the earls of Fife at the ceremonies of inauguration. One sub-contemporary account of James VI's coronation actually says that it was John, Earl of Atholl, who crowned the King, but the official account makes it clear that this is wrong. It was far too important to avoid any departure from recent precedent and to give no opportunity to those who might denounce the ceremony of 1567 as no true coronation. There was, besides, no difficulty about receiving the co-operation and the blessing of the Church—the Reformed Church. There was medieval precedent for a coronation sermon: for example, in 1390, after the coronation of Robert III at Scone,

The Bishope of Galloway thare, Thomas
(A theolog solempne he wes)
Made a sermound rycht plesand
And to the matere accordand.

In 1567 it was John Knox who 'made an excellent sermon before the coronation', taking 'a place of the scripture forthe of the bookes of the kinges, where Joas was crowned very yonge, to treate on'. But neither Knox nor any other mere minister was a suitable person to perform the ceremony of anointing, and indeed, it seems, Knox and the more extreme reformers repudiated the sacramental concept inherent in unction and would have preferred the omission of that act. According to the papal bull which had authorised the anointing of Scottish kings, unction was to be given by the Bishop of St Andrews, whom failing the Bishop of Glasgow. But in 1567 the Archbishop of St Andrews was John Hamilton, conservative in religion and a Marian in politics, and the Archbishop of Glasgow was a papalist who had been in France since 1560. Most of the other bishops in the kingdom were either of Roman Catholic sympathies or supporters of Queen Mary, or both. Even of the three bishops who had carried their support of the Reformation so far as to organise the Reformed Church in their dioceses, Alexander Gordon of Galloway was a Marian and Robert Stewart of Caithness was disqualified since he had never himself been consecrated. Adam Bothwell, Bishop of Orkney, alone was qualified and willing to act. He had been provided by the pope and consecrated in 1559, but had since been energetic on behalf of the Reformed Church. James VI was thus anointed by a duly consecrated bishop.

The coronation of the King, and the investing of him with the sword and sceptre, seem to have been shared by Bishop Bothwell and two of the superintendents of the Reformed Church—dignitaries who were equivalent to bishops in their administrative functions. Probably, while the Bishop placed the crown on the child's head, the sceptre and the sword were delivered by the two superintendents—John Erskine, superintendent of Angus, and John Spottiswoode, superintendent of Lothian (father of the Archbishop who was to crown Charles I).

Only then, it appears, did laymen intervene, and in circumstances arising from the extreme youth of the King. A child of a year old could not sit with a three-and-a-half-pound crown on his head to receive the homage of his nobles, and the crown was therefore held over his head by John Erskine, Earl of Mar, who was the boy's guardian and keeper of the royal person, while the nobles present came up and touched the symbol of kingship in token of their consent to James's inauguration. Nor could the child take a coronation oath in person, and one part of the proceedings at Stirling that day had been the taking of an oath on behalf of the new King by James Douglas, Earl of Morton, who was acting as leader of the King's party until the Earl of Moray, the Regent-designate, returned from France. The oath followed traditional lines, but its emphatic undertaking to root out all heretics and enemies to the true worship of God had a different meaning now from the undertaking to act against heretics which had been imposed by John XXII on the Scottish kings when he authorised their anointing.

James VI's minority was almost as troubled and eventful as any which had preceded it. His first Regent, the Earl of Moray, was assassinated in January 1570 and the second, the Earl of Lennox, was killed in a scuffle in September 1571. Civil war was going on intermittently between the supporters of the King and those of his mother, and the third Regent, the Earl of Mar, a man not ruthless enough for the times, died after little more than a year in office—because, it was said, he 'loved peace and could not have it'. Then came James Douglas, Earl of Morton, who succeeded in obtaining English help to batter down the defences of Mary's last stronghold, Edinburgh Castle, in May 1573, and then ruled unchallenged for several years during which the country enjoyed tranquillity. In the spring of 1578 some personal rivals of Morton persuaded the King, who was then approaching his twelfth birthday, to take authority nominally into his own hands. The regency thus came technically to an end, and from that point the government was carried on in the name of the King, but Morton soon regained control of affairs and kept it for another two years.

Serious though the troubles of the regencies were, it was one party—the King's party—which had so far succeeded in remaining in control and there had been far less of the unprincipled manœuvring for power which had marked previous minorities. It was only after Morton's fall in 1580 that something like the old pattern emerged, with a struggle for ascendancy between two factions. One of them—the conservatives—favoured an alliance with France or Spain, it was disposed to consider schemes whereby Mary would be restored to rule in partnership with her son, and it was lukewarm towards the Reformation; the other was ultra-Protestant in its religious outlook and anxious for a definite league with England.

It was in these circumstances that James first became of some political importance, if only as the instrument of first one faction, then another. In 1579 there arrived from France Esmé Stewart, seigneur d'Aubigny, who was a first cousin of Darnley and, after an aged great-uncle, James's nearest kinsman on his father's side. James had never known either his father or his mother, he had been starved of affection in his childhood and now, in his adolescence, he gave his whole-hearted devotion to his accomplished cousin from France, whom he created Earl, and later Duke, of Lennox. Esmé was probably concerned mainly with the purely personal ends of safeguarding his reversionary rights in the Scottish property of the Lennox Stewarts and in the place in the royal succession which that family had both as being heirs to Darnley and as standing after the Hamiltons in the succession to Mary. But he became a focus for the faction opposed to Morton, who was arrested at the end of 1580 and executed in 1581, and then he became a focus for those who were intriguing on behalf of Mary, the Roman Church and Spain. The alarm caused by the activities of foreign agents in Scotland led to a kind of Popish Scare, which Lennox's own profession of the Protestant faith did nothing to allay, and in August 1582 James was seized by the ultra-Protestant and pro-English faction in a *coup d'état* known as the Ruthven Raid. The Protestant Church, which had been highly suspicious of Lennox, applauded this 'act of reformation' as it was called. The King was forced to acquiesce in the banishment of Esmé, who died soon afterwards in France.

The government of the Ruthven Raiders lasted only a few months, for in June 1583 James escaped from them and a new administration was formed under James Stewart, who had been a lieutenant of Lennox and was created Earl of Arran. The Earl of Gowrie, who had headed the Ruthven Raiders, was executed, the lords who had supported him were banished to England and the Reformed Church was firmly subjected to the crown. At the end of 1585 the banished lords returned to bring about a *coup d'état* which overthrew Arran. A kind of coalition government was then formed, including men who had supported Arran as well as men who had supported the Ruthven Raid, and the leading place in it was soon taken by John Maitland of Thirlestane, who had been a member of the Queen's party during the civil war and had served in Arran's government, but now advocated a policy of conciliating the Presbyterians and maintaining friendly relations with England. By a treaty formulated under Arran and finally concluded in 1586, James became Elizabeth's pensioner and she undertook to do nothing to derogate from any title he might have to succeed her, unless she should be provoked by ingratitude. This was sufficient to ensure James's acquiescence in his mother's execution in 1587 and his friendly neutrality when the Spanish Armada sailed against England in 1588. Maitland of Thirlestane retained office, with some intermission, until his death in 1595, but he was neither a royal favourite in the sense that Esmé had been nor a dictator like Arran, and his position gradually approximated more and more to that of a prime minister. James attained the age of twenty-one in 1587, but at what point it came to be the King and not Maitland who really directed affairs it would be hard to determine. At any rate, it has been neatly said that Maitland, before his death, 'had trained a successor. His successor was the King himself.'*

Both of the conflicting Scottish factions had become less dangerous politically while Maitland was directing affairs than they had been in the days of Esmé Stewart and the Ruthven Raiders. The conservative or 'Roman Catholic' faction had lost some of its point with the execution of Mary in 1587, and its continued dealings with Spain could not now be represented as anything other than a bid to bring in foreign domination. Equally, the ultra-Protestant faction had a new orientation since the conclusion of the league with England in 1586, for it no longer re-

*Maurice Lee, *Maitland of Thirlestane*, 291

presented a line in foreign policy to which the Scottish government was not officially committed. It had also lost the aristocratic support it had once enjoyed, and now consisted essentially of the more outspoken Presbyterian ministers and such members of their flocks as they could influence. Thus its attempts to interfere in domestic and foreign policy looked like a bid for clerical domination. Maitland, and James after him, could therefore on the whole rely on patriotism and anti-clericalism as forces to strengthen their hands in an attempt at a kind of non-party rule based on the pursuit of a *via media*.

The turning-point of the reign came in 1595–6. Even with the support he could muster, James was not strong enough to challenge simultaneously the northern earls, who kept alive the conservative tradition and still intrigued with Spain, and the ultra-Protestants, who chided him for his leniency towards the Roman Catholics and felt that Scotland was not yet the monolithic example of godliness which they craved. The King therefore conciliated the Presbyterians by concessions, mostly of a non-material and revocable kind, and won their co-operation in a campaign against the northern magnates which convinced the latter that they must at least make a show of submission. From that point most of the 'Roman Catholics' conformed publicly, and nothing more was heard of Spanish intrigues. After thus destroying the political importance of one faction, the King moved against the other. In 1596 the ministers were going further than ever before in their criticism of the King, both for his public policies and his personal profanity, and Andrew Melville, the leader of the Presbyterian party, had a famous interview with his sovereign in which he plucked him by the sleeve and called him 'God's silly vassal'. These excesses gave the King a chance to demonstrate that public opinion was no longer behind the ministers as it once had been and that in particular they had lost the support of the people of the capital.

James then proceeded, by a series of ingenious manœuvrings, to break the domination which Andrew Melville and his party had established in the General Assembly and to weaken the position of the Assembly altogether. He saw to it that the Assembly, instead of consisting mainly of ministers from the areas in the south which were strongly influenced by Andrew Melville, should also contain representatives from the more conservative regions north of the Tay. He also used his statutory powers in connection with the summoning of Assemblies to interrupt the regular series of their meetings and indicate that, if necessary, he could dispense with an Assembly altogether. Stage by stage, he turned the Assembly into at least an acquiescent instrument of his policy, if not an enthusiastic or even a completely docile one, and by 1610 he had won its assent to the revival of the office of bishop. The bishops were to be royal agents in both Church and State.

As early as 1583, when he was only seventeen, James had declared his intention to be a 'universal king', standing above faction and selecting his advisers at his own will. At that stage it looked like an empty boast, but it was precisely the policy he was able to put into effect from 1596 onwards. He did select his advisers with uncommon skill, giving his preference to men of ability, irrespective of their birth, and professional administrators found unprecedented opportunities for careers in James's reign. There were courtiers, too, and personal favourites, but they played no part in affairs unless they had ability as well, and peers of ancient lineage were on the whole excluded likewise from much influence. The King was on familiar terms with many of his subjects, but his doings hardly recall those of James III and James V except to point a contrast. 'Jockie o' the sclates' was the Earl of Mar, who had been one of the King's schoolfellows and had distinguished himself in arithmetic, but the offices to which he was advanced were decorative rather than influential. 'Tam o' the Cowgate', by contrast, who came of a family of small lairds and burgesses, was at the centre of affairs as Lord Advocate and Secretary of State and became Earl of Haddington only in his later years.

James was the first of his line who was able to make use of his own chosen agents without thereby alienating the heads of the old noble houses. Part of the explanation lies in his own gifts of cajolery, part in the increasing prestige of the monarchy, but part in his skilful use of the patronage at his disposal. It was much to his advantage that he had at his disposal patronage on an unprecedented scale, thanks to the fact that developments before and since the Reformation had given the crown almost complete control over the vast properties of the Church. To have made an effective appropriation of all ecclesiastical lands directly to the crown would, of course, have antagonised as many men as a series of forfeitures would have antagonised. But the crown could confirm church properties to those who held them, it could give the holders a security of tenure which they had previously lacked, and above all it could convert holdings of church lands into heritable temporal lordships. Many noble families had been well entrenched in church lands since before the Reformation, and had retained those lands since, but it had always been felt that there was an element of impermanence in their position, and that sooner or later there would have to be a settlement which might deprive them of their gains. James asserted his right to dispose of such properties, but took care in practice not to disturb existing rights and made use of his powers to confer the security which comes from an hereditary title. Just how successful James was in thus winning the nobility was shown in the next generation, when Charles I, by threatening them with the loss of their church lands, alienated them and took a big step towards his own downfall.

James VI's success in establishing his domination over both the nobles and the Reformed Church was spectacular, but perhaps his most enduring achievement and the one which was to do most to shape the life of Scotland in later generations was his success in bringing about a new respect for law and order. Nobles who in any way challenged the crown, whether by pursuing private feuds or by maintaining private rights which seemed to infringe the sovereignty of the crown, were taught sharp lessons. The royal authority was extended as never before to the remote parts of the country. The problem of 'putting order on the Border' was an old one which had defeated James's predecessors, but, partly because he was able after 1603 to tackle the problem on an

Anglo-Scottish basis, he was able to reduce the frontier lands to a degree of ordered government never known before. In the Highlands, he put an end to the policy of raising up feudal magnates at the expense of clan chiefs, and relied instead on royal officials, including bishops, and on the clan chiefs themselves, whom he made responsible for the good behaviour of their clans. Orkney and Shetland, too, were firmly bonded into the Scottish realm as they had never been before.

James's practical measures to consolidate his kingdom and subject all estates of men in it to his own rule were supported by his theorising. Andrew Melville advanced the view that there were 'two kingdoms' in Scotland and that the kingship over one of them, the Church, belonged to Christ and to the General Assembly as His agent. James saw things differently. He believed in 'one kingdom', including both Church and State, with Christ as its Head and with King and parliament as His agents. In practical terms, this meant a contest between the General Assembly on one side and King-in-parliament on the other, but James's theorising about his responsibility to God and not to any intermediary contributed to a new view of monarchy which had developed since the Reformation. The reformers, in Scotland as elsewhere, had found it necessary to assert the divine right of kings in opposition to papal pretensions, and this led directly to the King's claim to be answerable to God alone and not to any of his subjects.

This all represented a very different state of opinion from that in which the Stewart dynasty had made its beginnings, with a purely statutory title to the throne, and the whole concept of the significance of the reigning line had undergone a change. After all, the succession had now been preserved in the Stewart family, throughout nine generations, in a manner sometimes so tenuous as to seem almost miraculous, and a novel sanctity attached to hereditary succession. The long series of over 100 Scottish Kings was now seen as a succession by right of blood, not by right of choice. This notion was to develop even further after James VI's time, and in 1685 it was possible for the Scottish parliament to boast of the 'sacred authority' of a 'sacred race' of 'glorious kings' under whom the nation had 'continued for upwards of two thousand years in the unaltered form of our monarchical government'. It was appropriate that in Charles II's reign the long gallery at Holyroodhouse was decorated with a series of alleged portraits of the entire succession, from Fergus I onwards. It was all a most profound change from the pedestrian and utilitarian view of the monarchy which had prevailed when Robert II became King.

James VI was the last of his dynasty to rule over Scotland as a separate kingdom, and his career not only concludes, but to some extent epitomises, the history of the Stewarts in Scotland. His personality and temperament, to begin with, were in contrast to those of most of his predecessors. One characteristic of the house, at least after its first two Kings, Robert II and Robert III, had been a kind of recklessness. James I and James II, and again James V, had been reckless in extending, beyond the point required by statesmanship, policies which were in themselves soundly enough conceived. James III, despite his reputation for timidity, had shown the same tendency in the severe action he took against Albany's supporters in 1484 and in his obvious blindness to the folly of alienating the nobility. James IV was reckless in battle if not in diplomacy and in internal policy. Mary was reckless and impulsive when she allowed her heart to rule her head.

James VI, by contrast, was the soul of caution. Constitutionally, he had a marked distaste for bloodshed or even for the sight of arms—possibly, it has been suggested, because of ante-natal experience, when the daggers of Rizzio's murderers flashed before his mother's eyes three months before his birth. His temperamental aversion from violent action of any kind owed something also to what he had seen with his own eyes in his minority. He may have remembered the murder of Moray, for he was then three and a half. He would certainly remember the alarm caused by the scuffle in Stirling in which the Regent Lennox was shot, for he was in Stirling Castle that night and by that time he had passed his fifth birthday. Besides, that incident would often be recalled by those who thought that it demonstrated the boy-king's wisdom: shortly before, the child had been taken to a meeting of parliament presided over by the Regent, and, his attention wandering to a hole in the tablecloth, he pronounced solemnly, 'There is a hole in this parliament', which was subsequently thought to have been prophetic. James was old enough to be taking an interest in affairs in 1573, when Edinburgh Castle was captured and the captain of the defenders was hanged.

If James had thus seen some of the results of violence, he had also had experiences which taught him something of the need to gain his ends by dissembling, perhaps even by trickery, certainly by diplomacy. His brief spell of happiness with Esmé Stewart had been rudely interrupted by the Ruthven Raiders, and at that point he may well have thought, as his mother said after the Rizzio murder, 'Enough of grief; I will study revenge'. He never forgave the lords who had taken his friend from him or the ministers who had supported their *coup*, and one of his first acts when he recovered his liberty was to bestow on Esmé's son some of the property which had been enjoyed by the father. But when James was still in the hands of the Raiders, he had no alternative but to appear to submit and to bide his time until they became less watchful over his movements. Later, it was only a man of unusual self-control who could have endured Andrew Melville's behaviour: what would Henry VIII have done to a cleric who called him 'God's silly vassal'? And James had also to cope with the antics of his wild cousin, Francis, Earl of Bothwell, who more than once forced his way into the royal apartments and had the King at his mercy. James had learned by hard experience that only caution and subtlety could prevail.

But, apart from his own first-hand experiences, James had studied Scottish history. His tutor, George Buchanan, was at work on a History of Scotland in the very years when he was teaching James. Buchanan had been the pamphleteer of the revolution of 1567 which deposed Mary and put James on the throne, but James reacted against his tutor's attempt to indoctrinate him with the argument that kings were responsible to their subjects. He would make up his own mind about the lessons of the past. His distaste for rebellion in any shape led him to distrust the ministers of the Reformed Church, who had been associated with the uprising against Mary of Guise in 1559–60; and Andrew Melville's attitude, added to the blessing given by the General Assembly to the Ruthven Raid, confirmed him in suspicion of clerical influence in any shape or form. He was to be a strong advocate of the restoration of the office of bishop, but he was emphatic that the bishops must not be like 'proud, papal bishops' and must be firmly subjected to himself as his agents for controlling the rank and file of the ministers. He was thus in no danger of falling under such a domination of clergy as had contributed to the downfall of James V.

James learned much from history about the nobles, too. He realised, perhaps more clearly than any of his predecessors, how regalities infringed and undermined royal authority. But he had also learned—and perhaps this was the most important lesson—that ruthless severity towards the nobles was fatal. Much as he disliked the nobles' franchises, he was far too wary to make a frontal attack on them and instead pursued a policy of infiltration by fostering jurisdictions under the crown which would compete with the judicial powers of the magnates. He knew, too, that the ultimate sanction which the crown had at its disposal in dealing with the nobles, namely forfeiture, was one to be used only sparingly. By policy as well as by temperament, therefore, his aim was conciliation, his object was to win rather than to repress. He was in no danger of falling into the errors of James I and James V.

One of the characteristics of a good many of the Stewart monarchs was an acquisitiveness which went beyond a statesmanlike desire to increase the resources of the crown. It is plain enough in James I and in James II. James III was described as 'wondrous covetous', and of James V it was said that 'this King inclineth daily more and more to covetousness'. James VI may have had the acquisitive instinct, but it was tempered by statesmanship. Whatever his motives, he did succeed in making regular taxation on a substantial scale a part of Scottish fiscal policy for the first time, and to that extent modernised Scottish administration. On the other hand, he used his control of ecclesiastical property less to enrich the crown than to appease the nobles and provide for the ministers and bishops of the Reformed Church. Besides, there is no reason to think that James would have wanted to hoard money. Like James III, James IV and James V he was a patron of builders and architects, and the evidence of his work can still be seen at Edinburgh Castle, at Linlithgow and at Dunfermline. He resembled James I in his interest in academic learning, and desired that the University of Edinburgh, founded in his minority, should be known as 'The Academy of King James'.

Another persistent characteristic of the line seems to have been a tendency to deteriorate with the passing of years. A sixteenth-century writer remarked that many people were accustomed to compare the Stewart Kings with the horses of the district of Mar, 'which in youth are good but in their old age bad'.* Signs of deterioration can be detected in James I and even in James II, though the latter died when he was no more than thirty. James III's record in his later years suggests something of the same kind of overweeningness which cast caution aside. In the case of James V, the remark that he was inclining daily more and more to covetousness itself suggests deterioration, and his life ended in what seems like mental and physical collapse. But deterioration with the passing of years is most marked in the reign of James VI. It was perhaps his misfortune that he lived to the age of almost fifty-nine, which made him an old man by Stewart standards. Indeed, when he died, his years exceeded those of every sovereign of his house except the first two, who came to the cares of kingship late in life, and the last—James VII and II—who was relieved of the burden of kingship by the Revolution of 1688.

If James VI had died twelve or fifteen years earlier than he did, the chances are that his repute would be higher. It has been said of him that he was more admirable in adversity than in prosperity,

*John Major, *Greater Britain* (Scottish History Society), 368

and it is certainly hard to reconcile some of the follies of his later years with his sure grasp of affairs in Scotland down to perhaps 1610 or 1612. He may not unreasonably have felt that his work was done and that he deserved some relaxation. But we cannot leave out of account the importance of his changed circumstances after 1603. In Scotland he had been faced with hostility, open criticism, plain-speaking, and neither his office nor his person had enjoyed complete security. In England he was surrounded by flattering courtiers and obsequious prelates, and even when the House of Commons criticised him it was apt also to use language which amounted to adulation. This all went to James's head, and, added to his lofty concept of the royal office as of divine institution, led him to believe that he could do no wrong and to lay aside his capacity to calculate.

The Scottish monarchy did not end with James VI. It continued until 1 May 1707, when, in terms of the Treaty of Union, the kingdom of England and the kingdom of Scotland alike came to an end, to be merged into a new United Kingdom of Great Britain. But much changed, both for Scotland and for its ruling house, on 24 March 1603, when the English heralds proclaimed: 'Forasmuch as it hath pleased Almighty God to call to His mercy out of this transitory life Our Sovereign Lady, the High and Mighty Princess Elizabeth, late Queen of England; by whose death the crown of this realm is now come to the High and Mighty Prince James the Sixth, King of Scotland, who is lineally and lawfully descended from the body of Margaret, the daughter of the High and Renowned Prince, Henry VII, King of England: We therefore publish and proclaim that the High and Mighty Prince James the Sixth, King of Scotland, is now become also our only lawful, lineal and rightful liege lord, James the First, King of England.'

Bibliography

Our knowledge of the history of the earlier Scottish kings is scanty because there is very little wholly reliable and strictly contemporary evidence for any period before the twelfth century. There are entries in Annals, especially Irish Annals, and there are chronicles and narratives composed at various dates, but it is always uncertain how far such writings may incorporate either earlier material which has since been lost or traditions with some foundation in fact. Nearly all of the material written before 1286 was collected by Alan Orr Anderson in *Early Sources of Scottish History* (2 vols, Edinburgh, 1922) and *Scottish Annals from English Chroniclers* (London, 1908). There were some important narrators who wrote in the later Middle Ages and preserved information about earlier centuries as well as their own times: John of Fordun (d. *c.*1384) and Walter Bower (d. 1449), whose works are combined in the *Scotichronicon* (ed. Goodall, 1759); Andrew Wyntoun (d. *c.*1420), whose *Orygynale Cronykil* was issued by the Scottish Text Society; and John Major, whose *History of Greater Britain*, originally published in 1521, was printed in translation by the Scottish History Society. All of those writers adhered to the conventional mythology about the origins of the Scottish nation and its monarchy, but the chief mythologist was Hector Boece (d. 1536), whose highly speculative *History* is available in various editions.

About the beginning of the twelfth century extant charters and other documents begin to occur sporadically, and their bulk increases fairly steadily from that point, so that historical writing has a surer basis. The earliest charters, down to 1153, were printed by Sir Archibald Lawrie, *Early Scottish Charters* (Glasgow, 1905); and royal charters for 1153–1214 are in G. W. S. Barrow, *The Acts of Malcolm IV* and *The Acts of William I* (Edinburgh 1960, 1971)—part of a series intended to reach 1424. With the fourteenth century we reach a stage at which official archives become available. Some financial records, and records of crown grants of lands, begin in the reign of Robert I; for acts of parliament there is no strictly official record until 1466, but there is much reliable information for a century and a half before that; the records of the council begin in the fifteenth century. The reign of James IV is perhaps the first for which the record evidence can be described as adequate, and for his reign, as well as for the end of his father's, there is an important, though over picturesque, narrative, in Robert Lindsay of Pitscottie, *History of Scotland* (Scottish Text Society and other editions). The official records mentioned above have been published by H.M.S.O.

Until the sixteenth century, however, our sources are still defective to the extent that they give little information about men's thoughts, and the motives lying behind policy can be only a matter of inference. It is only in the reign of Mary that a considerable quantity of informal correspondence is first extant, and to this there are presently added a number of diaries and memoirs. A mass of correspondence, mainly official, is printed in *Letters of James IV* (Scottish History Society), *Letters of James V* (H.M.S.O.), *Letters and Papers of Henry VIII* and *Calendar of State Papers relating to Scotland and Mary, Queen of Scots*. The less formal letters of Mary of Guise were published by the Scottish History Society, which also issued *Papal negotiations with Mary, Queen of Scots*. The most important memoirs are John Knox, *History of the Reformation in Scotland* (ed. D. Laing, 1846–8, and W. Croft Dickinson, 1949), and the *Memoirs of his own life* by Sir James Melville of Halhill (Bannatyne Club).

The principal books and articles in which scholars have made use of the sources can be reviewed in chronological sequence according to the periods with which they deal. William Forbes Skene, *Celtic Scotland*, vol. i (2nd edn, Edinburgh, 1886), has not yet been superseded as an account of the monarchy before 1100. William Douglas Simpson, *Dunstaffnage Castle and the Stone of Destiny* (Edinburgh, 1958), is a recent examination of some of the mythology. James Cooper, 'Four Scottish Coronations' (*Scottish Ecclesiological Society Transactions*, 1902), deals with the whole history of the coronation rite. R. L. G. Ritchie, *The Normans in Scotland* (Edinburgh, 1954), is an illuminating and spirited account of the transformation of Scottish society and institutions in the twelfth century and gives the earlier history of the families of Balliol, Bruce and Stewart. G. W. S. Barrow, *Robert Bruce* (London, 1965), is much more than a biography, and expounds the importance of the concept of 'the community of the realm'. A. A. M. Duncan, *Scotland: The Making of the Kingdom*, and Ranald Nicholson, *Scotland: The Later Middle Ages* (Edinburgh, 1975, 1974), cover the period to 1513.

With E. W. M. Balfour-Melville, *James I, King of Scots* (London, 1936), we come to a period where something like a rounded picture of a monarch and his policy can be presented. No similar work has yet been attempted for James II or James III, but for James II's reign and the early years of James III we can draw on the exhaustive researches of Annie I. Dunlop in her *James Kennedy, Bishop of St Andrews* (Edinburgh, 1950), and some account of James III is given in the first chapter of R. L. Mackie's scholarly and comprehensive *King James IV of Scotland* (Edinburgh, 1958).

From 1513, secondary books, like the sources, multiply. The most recent account of the reigns of James V, Mary and James VI is in G. Donaldson, *Scotland: James V to James VII* (Edinburgh, 1965), which has a full bibliography. The important negotiations surrounding the matrimonial projects of James V are related in E. Bapst, *Les mariages de Jacques V* (Paris, 1889). Of the many biographies of Mary, Queen of Scots, the best is probably now that by Antonia Fraser (London, 1969), but for any reader who wants to see a discussion of the original evidence the book to study is D. H. Fleming's *Mary, Queen of Scots* (London, 1898). Among the voluminous writings on the Kirk o' Field mystery, the works of R. H. Mahon advanced the theory of a conspiracy against Mary, and R. Gore-Browne's *Lord Bothwell* (London, 1937) has some ingenious argument on this subject. G. Donaldson, *The Scottish Reformation* (Cambridge, 1960), gives the ecclesiastical background to Mary's policy, and Maurice Lee's *James Stewart, Earl of Moray* (New York, 1953) is the best account of political developments.

For the reign of James VI, D. Harris Willson, *James VI and I* (London, 1956), is both readable and scholarly. Maurice Lee's *John Maitland of Thirlestane* (Princeton, 1959) explains the politics of the period when James was attaining maturity.

The principal documents for the whole history of the Scottish kingship are to be found, with connecting commentary, in *A Source Book of Scottish History*, ed. W. Croft Dickinson, G. Donaldson and I. A. Milne (3 vols, 2nd edn, Edinburgh, 1958–61). Sir Archibald Dunbar, *Scottish Kings* (2nd edn, Edinburgh, 1906), is the standard work for chronology. *The Scots Peerage*, ed. J. B. Paul (9 vols, 1904–14), is indispensable for the main facts about the great landed families, and I. F. Grant, *Social and Economic Development of Scotland before 1603* (Edinburgh, 1930), gives the necessary background to the financial and economic policy of the crown. R. S. Rait, *The Parliaments of Scotland* (Glasgow, 1924), is the principal work on constitutional history.

Index

The numerals in **bold type** refer to the figure-numbers of the illustrations